THE TABLET OF MY HEART:
Journal Writing for Spiritual Growth

THE TABLET OF MY HEART:

Journal Writing for Spiritual Growth

by
Ramona Czer

NORTHWESTERN PUBLISHING HOUSE
Milwaukee, Wisconsin

Cover design and art by Linda K. Loeffler
Calligraphy by Denise Anderson

Scripture taken from the
HOLY BIBLE, NEW INTERNATIONAL VERSION
Copyright © 1973, 1978, 1984 International Bible Society
Used by permission of Zondervan Bible Publishers.

Library of Congress Card
Northwestern Publishing House
1250 N. 113th St., Milwaukee, WI 53226-3284
© 1991 by Northwestern Publishing House
Printed in the United States of America
ISBN 0-8100-0382-1

DEDICATION

To the main characters in my journals who have loved
me, stretched me and given me plenty to write about:

Larry, Megan, Erin, Allison and Briana.

CONTENTS

INTRODUCTION   9

THE TABLET OF BEGINNING   13

    Keep a Journal If . . .   14

    Challenges and Rewards   19

    Judging a Book by Its Cover: A Dialog   25

    Where to Begin   29

    Laters into Nows   35

    Do It With All Your Might   39

THE TABLET OF SELF-EXPRESSION   43

    The Case of the Disappearing Writer's Block   44

    Clustering: A Magic Tool   48

    Taming Your Monster Critic   52

    Lists   57

    Divine Details   60

    Richness   63

    Recapturing Awe   68

    Remembering the Past   72

    Now the Eyes of My Eyes Are Opened   77

THE TABLET OF LEARNING   81

Do I Have a Book for You   82

The Examined Life   85

Love Letters   90

Music Lessons   94

Writing Down Your Dreams   101

THE TABLET OF LIVING   105

Slowing Down   106

You Have All the Time You Need   109

Travel Tips   116

The Maybe Mommy   121

How to Big Talk   124

Joy in Discomfort   128

The Touch of Death   133

The Creative Project Journal   136

THE TABLET OF SHARING   141

Memoirs of a Dishwasher   142

Journals as Alabaster Jars   147

Once upon a Miracle   152

The Tablet of My Heart   155

INTRODUCTION

I COME TO YOU HUMBLY WITH WORDS OF ENCOURAGEMENT. You can keep a journal. You can find the discipline, the creativity, the honesty inside yourself to write thousands of words uniquely yours. I know it's possible because I have done it, over and over again, scribbling in spiral notebooks, bound books and even on computer disks. I know something else too—you'll never regret the time and energy spent bent over the tablet of your heart.

When I was sixteen a classmate inadvertently gave me a priceless gift. Pam Beal walked, talked and breathed her Christian faith, which I marveled at even then. Though rather plain and quiet, she could look you right in the eye and tell you exactly what she had to say out of love for Jesus. One day, soon after I became acquainted with her, Pam invited me to her home, a tumbled down, converted cottage I discovered to be filled with clutter and an indescribable air of joy. Up in her attic bedroom she showed me something precious to her, a notebook she had started. I looked closely at it, intrigued. It included Bible passages that had moved her or pricked her conscience, quotes from people and sources she wanted to remember, hymn verses, self-written prayers and meditations on events and emotions. It was simply a hodgepodge of words that together symbolized the spiritual walk of Pamela Beal. I loved it!

"It's kind of strange that I never thought about keeping such a notebook," I said to her with chagrin. Not only did I, like Pam, long to walk more closely with Jesus, but ever since some second grade, stapled booklets of mine, I'd poured my creative impulses into writing poems, stories, you name it. Why, why, hadn't it occurred to me to delve deeply into the things of the Spirit, with my pen in hand?

Reflective the rest of that day, I went home to start my first spiritual journal. I didn't call it that then. It was just a small black ring-binder where I began to pour out my thoughts and feelings about what went on around and inside me. I jotted down Bible verses, sermon excerpts and quotes from books by Catherine Marshall, Brother Andrew and Corrie ten Boom. I admitted temptations and petty sins, confessing them with such youthful sincerity that even now when I reread the book, I am both embarrassed and inspired.

Then came college, marriage and the first baby. During those intellectually and emotionally draining years, I'd start a new journal, continue it for awhile and then give it up. It was hard to remain excited about writing when my journals seemed strangled with fears and inhibitions. Maybe it was reading and analyzing all that great literature in college, or maybe writing all those term papers, but somehow the joy of journal writing had departed. Sadder yet, I felt like my walk with my Friend and Savior was also suffering. My spiritual life didn't feel like an adventure any more like it had during those months and years of the small black notebook. It felt like plodding responsibility and being mired in the dailiness of life.

Then, praise God, through teaching a weekly creative writing class in my husband's Christian Day School classroom, I discovered some potent ideas about the correlation between attitude and writing output. The techniques I learned based on those ideas freed me from my writing inhibitions. They freed me from my need to write perfect sentences. They freed me from my tendency to play the perfect daughter, perfect wife and perfect mother role even in my journal. Surprisingly, not only did I start writing reams more and enjoying the process, but the quality also seemed to improve. Though the point of a journal is not to write powerful prose, if it happens, don't fight it! Someday perhaps the Lord can use those powerful words to influence others.

This book you hold in your hand would never have come into being if I had not learned how to write often and revealingly in my journals. Because I longed to help others experience the satisfaction and joys to be found in this kind of expression, because I longed to pass on some of those powerful techniques and ideas, I wrote this book much as I did my journals—one day at a time. I set aside time to jot down my thoughts and experiences, interspersing my words with quotes from others that had moved or helped me.

I wrote it like that for two reasons: I wanted you to get to know me as a real person who sympathizes with the messy, busy, often frantic walk of faith; and I wanted the writing itself to be uncontrived. How sad, I felt, if you put my book down with a sigh, thinking, "Ah, but I could never write like she does!" No, fellow sister or brother in the Lord, you cannot write like I do, nor should you. You should learn to write like yourself, the wonderful, one-of-a-kind person God envisions you to be through Christ's redemptive power.

When you decide to take up my challenge and begin a spiritual journal, at first it will not be easy. I won't pretend about that. At first, it will be very hard indeed. However, the first section of this book, "The Tablet of Beginning," is designed to ease you into journal writing, to make it seem fun and illuminating. I've included exercises at the end of each chapter, and I recommend you try them so your weak writing muscles can become conditioned gradually.

After that, I designed the sections to correspond to the different ways I've used my journals over the years. Sometimes I've used them to explore my own feelings and perceptions, my experiences and my ideas. You can find guidelines and revelations about how to use your journal that way also in the section called "The Tablet of Self-Expression." At other times I have predominantly used my journal as a Bible study and prayer notebook. For insights into that method, turn to the section called "The Tablet of Learning." Eventually, we must take what we've learned from all of our writing and apply it to our lives. For help with beginning that challenging assignment, turn to the chapter under "The Tablet of Living." Finally, after much writing, you may be ready to use the ability you've developed to reach out to others with your writing. I'll give you guidance there too with "The Tablet of Sharing."

In the verses right after the ones that inspired the title of this book, God commands us to "Trust in the LORD with all your heart and lean not on your own understanding; in all your ways acknowledge him, and he will make your paths straight" (Proverbs 3:5,6). Learning how to acknowledge him in all of our ways and learning how to write love and faithfulness on the tablet of our hearts, takes daily, concentrated effort. Our busy, stressful lives war against such effort. Journal writing, spiritual journal writing, however, will force you to sit down regularly before your Bible. It will encourage you to slow down and ponder God's word and your own reactions to it. It will teach you about your own emotions, sins and dreams. It will help you express yourself more easily about the things of the Spirit.

Many people who claim to follow Jesus today don't talk about his power in their lives, maybe out of fear or shyness or the modern habit of "minding our own business."

We need to practice speaking about our beliefs, and what better place to practice this heartfelt expression than in our journals?

All this practice takes patience. Give this idea some time. Soon you too will be on a spiritual adventure that ranges further and deeper than you thought possible. Please allow me to be your guide and encourager as we journey together.

THE TABLET
OF BEGINNING

*There is a vitality, a life-force, an
energy, a quickening that is translated
through you into action and because
there is only one of you in all time, this
expression is unique. And if you block it,
it will never exist through any other
medium and will be lost. The world will
not have it.*

Eleanor Cameron,
The Green and Burning Tree

Keep a Journal If . . .

Test everything. Hold on to the good.
1 Thessalonians 5:21

I'm glad God inspired Luke to include the story of Mary and Martha. Otherwise, how could I identify with the early Christian women? If all they did was breathe, think and dream of Jesus and his power in their lives, what hope is there for me? Luke tells a different story. At least one woman knew of my struggle to be saintly when it's 8:30 at night and dirty dishes taunt me from the kitchen, the kids need bathing, and I'm bone weary. She also knew the feeling of shrewish words in her mouth: "Why won't anyone help me?"Martha understood my same zealousness for a clean and orderly house, for a nutritious meal actually served hot. So what's wrong with a little order and a lack of germs? Nothing, but maybe there's nothing exceedingly good about it either. Scandalous! Am I a traitor to much of what womanhood has stood for these thousands of years? Have our priorities really been wrong all this time?

No, and Yes. No, because in Proverbs I see that God honors my simple duties: "She gets up while it is still dark; she provides food for her family. . . . She watches over the affairs of her household and does not eat the bread of idleness" (31:15,27). Our homely profession has definite worth in God's eyes. Nevertheless, my priorities sometimes get out of whack when I worry.

Worry is what displeases Jesus, what prompts him to say to Martha: "Martha, Martha . . . you are worried and upset about many things, but only one thing is needed" (Luke 10:41,42). I worry because I can't get the wrinkles out of my new "care-free" tablecloth. I worry because all the kids' winter clothes are packed away, it's 40 degrees out, and I haven't washed in days. I worry because an old friend is coming for dinner, and she never has Kool-Aid stains on her counter or unidentifiable green pools in her refrigerator drawers. I have found a way to ease my worry, however, to slow down and deepen, to become more like Mary who "has chosen what is better, and it will not be taken away from her" (10:42). My journal forces me to sit at the feet of my Lord daily and meditate on his words. Maybe that seems strange if you've always thought of a journal as a diary, a place to catalog events. I don't. I consider my journal a place to plumb my soul, to record my emotions and thoughts, and to learn from what I've recorded. Somehow, those shrewish complaints sound pretty silly when they're down on paper.

Sure, I still nag sometimes. I still have my Martha Days, especially if I let things go too long and then blame everybody else for the mess. But on those days when I need to be "clothed with strength and dignity," I turn to my journal, and it helps me to "laugh at the days to come" (Proverbs 31:25).

KEEP A JOURNAL IF YOU LONG TO SLOW DOWN
AND FOCUS ON YOUR LIFE IN JESUS

Maybe you imagine my primary reason for turning to journal writing is my love of writing. Writers write, right? Actually, though I have some of the qualities of an ivory tower "artiste"—such as needing some minutes of solitude each and every day—the enjoyment I get from communicating my ideas and passions to others disqualifies me. I thrill to speaking in front of others. Publishing articles and getting the occasional fan letter is a high for me. What does all that mean? I think it means that writing just for myself has not been what's kept me going, keeping journals all these years.

I keep a journal, even a spiritual journal, because I have an awful memory. I'm one of those people who

15

seem so forgiving to others. Do something cruel to me, say something you regret, and ten minutes later everything will be okay because I won't be able to remember much anyway. When I'm having a minor argument with my husband, sometimes I say, "What about all those other times you did this same thing?"

"Name one time," he'll challenge. I can't, and guess who wins the argument?

I'm not trying to be facetious. Though being forgiving is also a blessing, my tendency to forget names, chronology and details bothers me. For a writer, in fact, it's disastrous. That's the very thing that brings a scene or explanation to life on the page—details! So now you know one of my main motivations in keeping a journal. I do so in order to capture forever what has moved me, intrigued me, changed me. I do so to note dates and experiences that otherwise would slip away into the mists of my mind. I do so because I also want to remind myself what my Lord has taught me in the past with this struggle or that answer to prayer. My journal helps me relax and enjoy my encounters more thoroughly. Instead of needing to scold myself over and over, "Remember this, Ramona. Hold on to it," I know my journal can take over that responsibility for me.

KEEP A JOURNAL IF YOU NEED HELP RE-MEMBERING BOTH THE DETAILS AND THE ATMOSPHERE OF YOUR CHANGING LIFE

One other strong reason reminds me almost daily to take up my pen. I need help knowing what I mean. I'm one of those people who thinks as I talk. I may start out with only the vaguest idea of what I think and believe, but gradually as the words tumble out it all gets clearer. "How do I know what I mean until I say it?" a young girl once said. Of course that means that I've been labeled "talkative" by many people. Not everyone is patient with those of us who babble on and on, digressing here, elaborating there. Sometimes they even view us as indecisive air-heads.

To help me understand all of my thoughts and feelings, then, I turn to my journals. I pre-think what I mean. I confront issues that I have strong feelings on, especially so that when the time comes, I have something clearly thought out to express. A great side benefit to this babbling on paper is that you can change your mind as many times as you want, and only God knows you haven't a clue yet what you really think. I believe that many people make up their minds too quickly on important matters merely because they're afraid to sound undecided or nonauthoritative. Don't fall into that trap. Take the time in your journal to get to know yourself.

KEEP A JOURNAL IF YOU WANT TO UNDERSTAND YOUR UNIQUE THOUGHTS AND FEELINGS

A few more good reasons to keep a journal:

KEEP A JOURNAL IF YOU WANT TO LEARN TO PRAY HONESTLY AND COMPLETELY

KEEP A JOURNAL IF YOU WANT TO EXERCISE YOUR POWERS OF OBSERVATION

KEEP A JOURNAL IF YOU HAVE STRONG EMOTIONS YOU NEED TO WORK THROUGH

KEEP A JOURNAL IF YOU NEED TO DISCOVER YOUR GOALS AND MAKE PLANS TO PURSUE THEM

KEEP A JOURNAL IF YOU WANT TO HAVE A RICH MOMENTO TO PASS ON TO YOUR DESCENDENTS

KEEP A JOURNAL IF YOU HOPE TO WRITE SOMEDAY FOR OTHERS

It's important to think about why you picked up this book in the first place. What do you hope to get out of journal writing? Life is too short, especially from the

Christian perspective that countless souls need to be saved, for dabbling in time- and energy-wasting pursuits. You need to know why this activity appeals to you. Then, on those days when the writing seems like an onerous chore, you'll have a good reason to keep going. If you like you can even borrow the following quote by William Stafford. Tack it up on a bulletin board over your desk and reread it when you wonder, "Why am I doing this?"

> Writing itself is one of the great, free human activities. There is scope for individuality, and elation, and discovery. In writing, for the person who follows with trust and forgiveness what occurs to him, the world remains always ready and deep, an inexhaustible environment, with the combined vividness of an actuality and the flexibility of a dream. Working back and forth between experience and thought, writers have more than space and time can offer. They have the whole unexplored realm of human vision.

> William Stafford,
> *Writing the Australian Crawl*

Choosing what is better, sitting at Christ's feet daily to learn from him and from yourself, will reward you. I promise. But now it's time to stop taking my word for it and go to find out for yourself.

Your Turn—Try to come up with one more reason I haven't mentioned, a personal one. Or elaborate on one of the reasons I listed. Why do you want to keep a journal? Give yourself a reason to begin.

Challenges and Rewards

My son, do not forget my teaching, but keep my commands in your heart, for they will prolong your life many years and bring you prosperity. Let love and faithfulness never leave you; bind them around your neck, write them on the tablet of your heart. Then you will win favor and a good name in the sight of God and man. Trust in the LORD with all your heart and lean not on your own understanding; in all your ways acknowledge him, and he will make your paths straight.

Proverbs 3:1-6

This Proverb issues challenges for the heart from God: Keep my commands in your heart. Write love and faithfulness on your heart. Trust in me with all your heart. Hard challenges, but ones with amazing promises attached: long life, a good name and, best of all, straight paths. How can we reap such results, however, if our hearts instead are far from God?

Ever since a pre-teen, I knew that the secret of staying close to my Savior must lie in Bible study. I knew that my salvation didn't depend on anything I did or didn't do—that's the wondrous claim only Christianity can make. But my sense of growing stronger in Christ, of being more able to withstand temptations and to be a light to others, was inextricably bound up with his word.

At age ten, I had read a book called *Rainbow Garden* where the heroine discovered the fullness of joy in Jesus and then matured in her faith through daily Bible reading. Since all she'd done was copy down verses that seemed especially meaningful to her in a special note-book, I thought, "I could do that too," and so started my own Bible notebook.

Then in my junior year in high school I met Pam Beal, the classmate who inspired me to begin a deeper kind of journal. I began to join my passion to learn more of Jesus with my passion to express myself in writing. The dedication verse I put on the first page of that journal is still a favorite of mine: "'Come, follow me,' Jesus said, 'and I will make you fishers of men.'" It symbolized my hopes for the notebook. I hoped that it would help me learn how to follow Jesus closely, how to leave behind the nets of my selfish preoccupations and delve into his word with renewed excitement. I hoped it would help me share my faith with others, encouraging them also to follow Jesus, a lot to expect from a small black book! Funny, for as long as I wrote in it, it delivered.

My Christian life has had its peaks and valleys. As I look back on it, I see that almost invariably the times when I walked most confidently, prayed most easily and often, were also the times when I wrote in my spiri-tual journal regularly. One valley came during the early years of my marriage. In the excitement and upheaval of a new baby and new bills, I wrote little. I also studied my Bible seldom. How I regret that now, for the apostle Paul says, "Everything that was written in the past was written to teach us, so that through endurance and the encouragement of the Scriptures we might have hope" (Romans 15:4).

Not only was I missing out on the hope Bible study and journal writing would have increased in me, but also on joy and direction: "The precepts of the LORD are right, giving joy to the heart" (Psalm 19:8); "Your word is a lamp to my feet and a light for my path" (Psalm 119:105).

Again Jesus finally made me realize what had been missing in my life and turned me back to his word. I began to write down once more all my longings, my thankfulness, even the questions that burned in my heart. It felt good! Yes, I'd been a Christian all along, saved by Christ's redemptive blood (faith isn't dependent on my feeling saved); but God made me an emotional being. He could have created me Spock-like if he had wanted to. Instead, he chose to give me these emotions which I in turn must surrender to him, daily, hourly. That process of surrendering everything, my worries and my joys, my experiences and my feelings, is what a spiritual journal is all about. It's such a thrilling and a comforting process that I long to share it with you.

What is a "spiritual journal"? I define it as a journal kept by a spiritual person. I don't always write about spiritual matters. Sometimes I talk about my editorial work or my struggle to learn a new sonata on the piano. It would be difficult to make letter writing or Beethoven sound innately spiritual, and yet everything a person who is turned toward God says and does reflects God's outlook. Or so it should be. My spiritual journal is my Bible study notebook, my notebook of self-expression, my prayer book, my daily cataloging of my life. It is where I speak of things that trouble me and where I dwell on God's words that seem to speak to me. At times I've used a divided loose-leaf binder for my journal, so that I can keep my Bible journal entries separate from my daily, more expressive entries. However, most of my journal writing life I've used a more organic journal with meditations on 1 John right next to complaints about what to do about a careless babysitter. Organic journals have their own charm. When you reread them, they astound you with how the mind works, and how your emotions color your decisions. Because I'd read in 1 John 3:18, "Dear children, let us not love with words or tongue but with actions and in truth," I decided to confront the babysitter with love-based suggestions rather than just never to call her again.

Many times my organic journals reveal the subtle interplay between what I am reading and learning and what I think and do. You may prefer, however, to have your Bible journal entries separate rather than all jumbled in with everything else. It's certainly easier, then, to find topics later. Ultimately, you must decide for yourself. Nothing says that you can't experiment and change your mind often. I suspect I'm not done yet developing the best system for my journal writing.

The benefits of Bible study are probably obvious to you, but what are the benefits of a Bible journal? When you add your own comments and experiences to your study, you surpass mere knowledge, and internalize it in the depth of your being. It becomes yours. I think that's what Paul meant when he made this ardent wish for the Christians in Ephesus:

> I pray that out of his glorious riches he may strengthen you with power through his Spirit in your inner being, so that Christ may dwell in your hearts through faith. And I pray that you, being rooted and established in love, may have power, together with all the saints, to grasp how wide and long and high and deep is the love of Christ, and to know this love that surpasses knowledge—that you may be filled to the measure of all the fullness of God (Ephesians 3:16-19).

Knowing something with our minds and knowing it with our hearts are two different things. Paul says this earlier in his letter: "I pray also that the eyes of your heart may be enlightened in order that you may know the hope to which he has called you, the riches of his glorious inheritance in the saints, and his incomparably great power for us who believe" (Ephesians 1:18,19).

When we apply God's word to what we are living, we set in motion the potential for great power in our lives.

I've felt it. When I truly dwell on the Lord's words, consider how they can change me or how I can use them to comfort, warn or inspire others, then trusting, loving and keeping his commands seem much easier. His power fills me. It's nothing I've done. It's his Spirit working in and through me. It's the Lord being with me as he promised:

> Do not let this Book of the Law depart from your mouth; meditate on it day and night, so that you may be careful to do everything written in it. Then you will be prosperous and successful. Have I not commanded you? Be strong and courageous. Do not be terrified; do not be discouraged, for the LORD your God will be with you wherever you go (Joshua 1:8,9).

So God issues heart challenges with wonderful promises and rewards. Why take a chance on missing out on a rich spiritual life when what he asks is so easy, namely, simple study and meditation. It's only hard at the very beginning. Soon you'll find yourself leaving more and more time for your spiritual journal because you love doing it. You love examining your life, God's word and your spiritual climate.

Trust me. It's true. What you are doing is storing up God's commands, calling out for insight and searching for hidden treasure (Proverbs 2:1-6). In return, he promises this: "then you will understand the fear of the LORD and find the knowledge of God. For the LORD gives wisdom, and from his mouth come knowledge and understanding" (Proverbs 2:5,6).

Yes. it will require something from you. You will have to slow down, deepen and choose what is better, what will not be taken from you (Luke 10:42). But the love and faithfulness you will gain in your closer walk with

God will be bound to you. You will write them down forever on the tablet of your heart.

Your Turn—At the end of each chapter, you will find suggested assignments, because you can read repeatedly what I have to say, but you won't experience the rewards of a closer walk with your Lord until you start writing yourself. So here's your first assignment: before you buy a notebook, before you read any further, define for yourself what a spiritual journal is. Write your opinion down on paper so you have to commit. You may change your mind later as you read or after you begin to write more and more. That's fine. But at least you will have some idea what this thing called journal writing, for a Christian, is all about.

Judging a Book by Its Cover: A Dialog

My First Diary: Hey, was I really so bad?

Me: Do you want an honest answer?

Diary: I think so.

Me: Okay, but don't blame me if it's not what you want to hear.

Diary: I was a gift from your mother, you ungrateful wench! You'd better be careful!

Me: Yes, I know, and she just gave me what I thought I wanted. What does a sixth-grader know? But I'll give my own daughters a very different kind of diary, one with room for their wholeness.

Diary: How cruel! Wasn't I beautiful? Green imitation leather, gilt-edged, with a gold lock and two tiny keys, lined pages, dated for your organizational pleasure. How can you say I wasn't perfect?

Me: Oh, but you were perfect—for the life of a flea! Each dated page was divided into five sections, one for every June 6th that would occur for the next five years. Since each page measured about 5 x 3 inches, that left me about 1 x 3 inches to record the story of my daily existence. I am not that small! Plus, when I did skip a page or ten, I felt so guilty. All those white, wasted pages staring at me accusingly!

Diary: If you're so smart, what's your idea of the perfect diary?

Me: I'm so glad you asked.

—Bound, like you were, so that my inner critic isn't tempted to rip pages out, or sometimes loose leaf, if I'm accustomed to writing without restraint, so I can organize some of my thoughts later.

—Large enough to let my hand move easily across the page. I've discovered that purse-size books cramp my style, and take up way too much room in my purse!

—Unlined, if possible. I like seeing how my penmanship is affected by my moods, how it goes uphill sometimes or becomes large and graceful when I'm feeling expansive. This is another expression of me—a visual revelation. Plus then I can easily doodle or draw in it.

—Nice, but not too nice—somewhere between attractive and gorgeous. I want to be proud of it, to enjoy handling it, but I don't want to be intimidated by it, thinking, "Oh, I have to write beautiful thoughts in such a beautiful book."

—Undated pages, for the joy in filling them when I want, as many pages at a time as I want. I will date my entries, however, so I have a chronological record of what I thought and experienced. (Then, when someone asks, "When was the winter of that amazing snowstorm," I will be the one who can prove her answer.) I also don't want the gaps in my diary that inevitably happen when things get hectic. Dated pages stare at you with their accusing blankness. Undated pages forgive you and take what you can give the next time.

—A bargain. I have often used sketch books picked up at toy stores on sale. That way, I can fool my inner critic again: "I can write anything I want to in a book that costs only $2!"

Diary:	How depressing! Is there anybody out there I would be perfect for?
Me:	Sure, there might be. What makes me feel joyful and uninhibited may make my next door neighbor uncomfortable and insecure. Journal writers have to find the right book for them.
	I've used big, medium and small size loose-leaf notebooks, spirals and heavier sketch pad spirals, and many different kinds of bound books. People could even write their journal entries on scraps of paper and stick them in file folders or throw them off a bridge into the Mississippi River if that's what makes them happiest. I've even heard of journal writers who pour their heart out onto computer disks. I can finally compose on a computer for some projects, but I prefer the intimate tactile feel of a paper and pen when I pour out in my journals. Some people may even want to own a diary much like you. They may like knowing exactly how much they are expected to write each day, they may like the pretense of security a tiny lock gives them, and they may like dated pages forcing them to write daily. That's good too, because whatever they write, no matter how little, will teach them and will record thoughts and moments that would otherwise be lost.
Diary:	Good. I feel better. Maybe my life isn't a waste.
Me:	Please don't say that! You served a very valuable function for me. You taught me

what I did want and need in a journal. In fact, because of you, I knew how many words inside me longed to spill out, pages and pages and pages of them. If my mother had never given you to me on that long-ago eleventh birthday, I might never have discovered the joy of journal writing. Thank you, my first diary, for that!

Your Turn—Write a description in your journal of "My Idea of the Perfect Journal." If your present journal doesn't measure up, tell why. When you fill it up, you'll then have an excellent idea of what kind to pick out for volume two of your collected journals.

Where to Begin

For we do not have a high priest who is unable to sympathize with our weaknesses, but we have one who has been tempted in every way, just as we are—yet was without sin. Let us then approach the throne of grace with confidence, so that we may receive mercy and find grace to help us in our time of need.
Hebrews 4:15,16

Beginning. It's a hard thing. Think of that first sit-up or that first lunge out of sleep-warm blankets. I'm afraid of beginnings, maybe because if I don't begin, I can't fail.

That makes sense, but it's also sad. Doesn't God tell us in this Hebrews passage to approach him with confidence and that, when we do, we will receive help for our problems? Perhaps if we approach our spiritual journals also with confidence they too will reward us more richly. But that can't happen if we believe we're always supposed to write glowing, taut and admirable prose. That's egotism, hobbling egotism, which says, "You must always be the best."

I used to think that way about my journals and other kinds of writing I would do. I wanted it to be beautiful, polished and publishable right away. I had no patience, and I also had little writing. "If it can't be perfect, why bother?" was my attitude.

I believe now that was a sinful attitude, even if it does smack of the old saw our parents told us, "Anything worth doing is worth doing right." Yes, but sometimes, you have to do it any way you can in order to learn and grow. It's like never giving to church because you can't manage a tithe, or never witnessing to your neighbor across the alley, because you always wanted to be a missionary in Africa. Through Christ, God loves us just as we are right now—he is able "to sympathize with our weaknesses."

I've learned to start any way I can, to sneak up on beginning by pretending it doesn't matter what I write or how I bungle an attempt to express my faith, because later God and I can work on it together. Together we can revise, spruce it up, give an extra five dollars, or add more next time to that awkward conversation over the fence. Christianity and writing are both processes, not destinations. If you think you have to wait to start a journal until you take a refresher course in grammar or even in "Creative Writing"—poppycock! Don't indulge in false modesty or wallow in self-pity. No one else is going to read your thoughts—so who cares what you write? Or, if someday your grandchildren find your journals and, charmed by your words, attempt to publish them, then an editor will do his job. Until then, your job is to engage, to approach the task with confidence, to pour out.

I do suggest these ways to help you begin. They've helped me many times in the past, and they still help me when I'm tempted to hold off beginning for whatever reason.

1. Write fast. Don't reread until your hand is exhausted.

2. Keep a list in your journal of possible topics—either on the first page or on a loose piece of paper you keep nearby—then consult it whenever your mind seems blank.

3. Time yourself for a set number of minutes (fifteen should be easy to do right away), and then force yourself to write continuously until the buzzer sounds. No fair looking back at what you've written, daydreaming, or even picking up your hand. Just write whatever is in your head, even if nothing is in your head. You may end up just writing about

how awful it is to keep writing. That's okay. You'll get sick of that subject soon enough and go on to others. I've done this exercise often, sometimes writing for as long as a half-hour non-stop, and I'm always amazed at what's inside my head that never would have been born on paper if I hadn't forced myself to write.

4. Pick an argument with yourself about your journal, ("I hate this!" "No, you don't.") and write it in dialog form. Keep going until you find out what your real inhibitions are.

5. Write your journal as a letter to someone you love and write or talk to often. Since this will seem natural to you, words should come easily.

6. Reread a short story, a poem or a Bible passage that you enjoy immensely. Write from the energy you feel immediately after putting it down.

7. Write about what moves you. Always find these subjects—they are your true ones, the ones that blossom under your pen, that make you start breathing fast as you write.

Peggy Curry tells how you can know which ones they are: "In the life of a writer, the heart must be moved, the mind teased, the imagination nurtured to that sharpness that makes the unforgettable click below the surface of thinking, the click that says somewhere far below what we take for granted, 'Hold onto this; let it fasten to you forever.'"

Sit quietly before your desk, hands in your lap. Now, slowly let your mind wander back over your day, or your yesterday. Relive it. What stands out? What made you angry or ashamed or enraptured? Go deep-sea fishing, don't just hug the shore. When you've discovered the thing you want to remember, to hold on to, pick up your pencil and fasten it to your journal forever.

8. Whenever you feel unsure of yourself, say this out loud, "I cannot do this wrong. Anything goes in my journal. I can blabber, I can sing, I can groan, I can shout. If I want, I can misspell words, I can misuse the English language, or write one single word over and over. I can write in words as big as my page or so tiny they're illegible. I can write as slowly, as fast, as dark, or as delicately as my mood dictates. I can write poems, accident reports, prayers or drivel. It doesn't matter, for here I am free to be me, the me of the moment. This book is mine. I am the only teacher, the only student, the only reader, the only writer. I begin now to set down anything, but anything is always something. It is me!"

9. Write at strange moments. Grab a pen as you wait for the suds to foam up in the kitchen sink. Write on your lap as your kids splash in the tub. Write in the car at stop-lights or during half-time at your son's basketball games. Sneak up on the writing and you'll surprise yourself at all you can say in odd moments, in odd places.

10. Touch on feelings and let the facts come in where they must to explain the feelings. Shed as many masks as you can to find out the real you, to confess what needs to be confessed, to reveal problems that need to be faced. Not only will this be stimulating, it will help you spiritually. You will find you can recognize your sins for what they are (on paper our excuses and posturing look pretty lame). You can then repent and ask for guidance. Your journal can easily become a way to ready yourself for heartfelt prayer.

11. If you're still having trouble, begin from the present moment and ask yourself these questions:

   a. Where am I in my life now?

   b. What am I thinking, feeling or experiencing?

c. What do I desire more than anything else?

d. Whom do I care about?

e. What is changing in my life?

f. What is changing inside me?

Write an evocative self-portrait based on your answers to these questions.

12. Or use these forms to tease your imagination into starting up:

a. A dialog with an idea (like "loneliness" or "holiness") or with God, yourself, your parents, objects, memories, ancestors, etc.

b. Prayer lists: who, what and why

c. Memories that are vivid in your mind (but may not be later—capture them NOW)

d. Witnessing experiences

e. Your goals

f. Quotes you like and why

g. Reading encounters (books, stories, poems, you want to remember)

h. T.V. shows and movies you like and why

i. Favorite Bible passages, memorable sermons or discussions

j. People you admire and why

k. Lists: what makes you afraid, gives you joy, or irritates you; what you believe or don't believe; what brings you peace; etc.

l. Unsent letters

m. Descriptions of people, places, and things

n. A chance to finish that conversation (what you wished you'd said)

o. I wish . . . (for yourself or others)

p. Heaven fantasies (what do you imagine it will be like?)

q. The table of contents for your autobiography
r. An incident told from another person's point of view (or even from a non-human point of view: like the argument you had with your husband as witnessed by your goldfish!)
s. Jokes or anecdotes you want to remember
t. The stepping-stones of your life
u. Draw a picture, doodle, or make a design

All that's left to do is begin. Remember this quote, or even tack it on a bulletin board over your desk as I do:

> Are you in earnest?
> Seize this very minute!
> What you can do, or dream you can,
> Begin it!
> Boldness has genius, power
> and magic in it.
> Only engage, and then
> the mind grows heated.
> BEGIN, and then the work
> will be completed.
>
> Goethe

Your Turn—Copy a similar list as mine into your journal. Be sure to leave room for additions as your own ideas emerge. Then choose one of the ideas and write for fifteen minutes nonstop. Do this to discipline yourself and to teach yourself that there is plenty in there to express if you simply turn the faucet on.

L aters into Nows

"At the time of the banquet he sent his servant to tell those who had been invited, 'Come, for everything is now ready.' But they all alike began to make excuses. The first said, 'I have just bought a field, and I must go and see it. Please excuse me.'"
Luke 14:17,18

There's no point in putting off beginning a journal because, not only is it good for you, it's fun! So why do we always wait? "Later," I've said too often, "later, I'll really delve into the Bible. Later, I'll get into the habit of writing every day. This week the kids are sick, and finances aren't what they should be. How can I concentrate with three pre-schoolers in the house? Later, when they're all in school, then I'll write and study and become a 'real' Christian."

A woman long ago wanted desperately to write. Teachers had told her as a girl that she had great talent. She believed them. But this was the century before ours so she bore many children and put in long hours of washing, baking, cleaning and sewing. Finding time to write seemed impossible. She kept the dream alive instead by saving every scrap of paper she could: used envelopes, the backs of receipts and letters, labels, anything. "Someday," she told herself, "I'll write down all my longings, my thoughts and my musings on these scraps of paper in my drawer."

She grew older, the children all left. At last she opened that drawer and drew out that pile of waiting blank paper. She sat there, though, just staring at all that blank paper, feeling just as empty. Where was it all, all she felt passionate about sharing? Somehow, tragically, the words were lost now; the talent, unused, had evaporated while she slaved over doing the right things. She had wasted her dream.

I believe the same thing can happen in our spiritual lives. We can ride only so long on our Sunday School knowledge, on our confirmation class cramming, or, if we were so blessed, our Christian high school or college enthusiasm. Eventually, the stories, the verses, the prayerful habit and the spiritual mind-set fade unless we rejuvenate them with new understandings learned at the feet of Jesus, our today-master. I know because I've had long famines in my spiritual life, times when I smugly said, "Later."

A few months ago at an evangelism meeting my pastor asked for a proof passage from one of us. My mind went blank. "What's wrong with me?" I thought. "I did better fifteen years ago in his confirmation class?"

I knew what was wrong. Somehow once again I'd let myself fall away from regular Bible study. Nothing could come to my lips that wasn't first roaming in my mind and heart. I hung my head as someone else produced the passage, and silently I asked God for forgiveness. Another rededication took place that night, another chance to discover the hard joy of being a Christian.

Sure, it's hard. And journal writing is hard. I've never claimed either one was easy, but whoever said being an adult Christian should be any easier than all that studying and memorizing we did as children. Something tells me I need an even stronger armor now than I did then, so I better be ready to carry it's heaviness. But there's joy in that too. Jesus is my squire, there to carry that heavy armor for me.

Now that I'm back into Bible study, I wonder why did I wait. Discovery, illumination comes every day, and I feel passionate again about learning, full of passages that touch and comfort me, no longer only lukewarm in my faith. I'm not saying the siren voice murmuring "Later" won't return, but now I've thought of a verse I can shout at it: Jesus says, "Seek first his kingdom and his righteousness. . . ." Matthew 6:33).

Stop saying "Later" to the urge to write in your journal too. If you don't, perhaps one day you'll feel like this woman.

Death in the Womb
by Lavelle Leahey

I have forgotten many poems
Because I slept when they were to be born.
For the dark hid me and made me safe.
And time, whose minutes became seasons—
As I wrapped defeat warmly on my shoulders—
Slid under the door behind the drapes
And mocking birds mock me in the spring
As I carry my stillborn poems in my womb.

Start now to turn all your laters into nows. Write down in your journal those goals you've been saving up to work on later. Later, you'll lose ten pounds. Later, you'll talk to your neighbor about Jesus' impact on your life. Then prayerfully commit those goals into God's hands now. Ask him in writing to help you stop procrastinating. When He says "Take no thought for tomorrow," I believe he also means to live today to the fullest, doing now the activities worthy of your calling as a child of God.

Maybe those chocolate chip cookies won't get baked or the windows washed, or maybe you can't be the President of the Ladies Club and a room mother, a part-time secretary and everything you have to be at home. Maybe you'll have to spend more time at Jesus' feet, more time bringing your children into the warmth of his presence, than the Marthas of this world will understand. But I believe that once Martha dried her hands and stopped grumbling over her meal preparation, once she really listened, the tightness eased in her. Later became now and peace filled her. "Now is the day of salvation" (2 Corinthians 6:2).

Your Turn—Write a letter to yourself about all the things you've been putting off that are important to you. Include mostly "Mary" activities, rather than "Martha" ones. Talk about why you've been avoiding doing what you long to and how that can all be changed.

Now is the time! How fast the moments fly!
How soon each hour is gone! Ye virgins, hear
And heed the midnight cry; Look for the break of dawn.
The Bridegroom comes; prepare to greet him!
Rise! Trim your lamps! Go out to meet him!
Now is the time! Now is the time!

TLH #509, v. 3

Do It with All Your Might

*"Whatever your hand finds to do, do it
with all your might. . . ."*

Ecclesiastes 9:10

You have your notebook and you want to write now,
not later; but maybe you're still wondering, "What do I
write about?" Don't think so hard! Write about what you
care about. Not only will that be more fun for you, but it
will make the words strong with meaning. Write about
the feelings and facts that bring tears to your eyes, the
experiences that even in memory make you laugh.
Write down the prayers of your frightened midnights,
the exulted rush of triumph you feel when your child
shows real love. Write about your favorite Bible passages, the ones you didn't even have to memorize
because their words seem to mingle with your thoughts
like salt in ocean water, making you what you are.

The important thing is passion. Keep the passion.
"Laid back Lutherans," my denomination is often accused of being, and though tranquillity is an important
quality of a Christian, so is energy. John Gardner, the
late and great writing teacher, says, "We care about what
we know and might possibly lose (or have already lost),
dislike that which threatens what we care about, and
feel indifferent toward that which has no visible bearing
on our safety or the safety of the people and things we
love." Perhaps by our laid-back, passive outlook, we
Christians are actually communicating to the world,
"We don't really care that you're dying in your sins."

A professor directly affected me my freshman year in
college with a parable he told:

There was a beautiful park with a wide paved pathway leading through it and then disappearing over a hill. You are travelling on a much narrower, more winding path. Soon you discover to your horror that the other path, the wide one, really leads to a huge pit of darkness that can't be seen at all until it's too late. You run back into the park and see hordes of leisurely picnickers walking, strolling up that lovely path to their doom. What do you do? Do you simply pack your gear, load your kids in the station wagon, and leave with a shrug? Or do you warn those picnickers, pulling them away from that path with all of your eloquence and ingenuity? You must decide, because even as we wait here, one by one more people are dropping over that edge into the deep chasm of eternity.

I am a naturally passive person. "Oh well," I try to assure myself, "someone else will probably tell them."

God, however, will not allow such laziness: "I know your deeds, that you are neither cold nor hot. I wish you were either one or the other! So, because you are lukewarm—neither hot nor cold—I am about to spit you out of my mouth" (Revelation 3:15,16). I know I'm nauseated when drinking lukewarm water. I imagine Jesus feels the same way about our lukewarm, passion-less spirituality.

Don't be afraid to pick the important topics, then, the ones you feel most passionate about, "to explore the rugged edge of your thought," as Natalie Goldberg says. She goes on to tell about how to start writing, "Let go of everything when you write, and try at a simple beginning with simple words to express what you have inside. It won't begin smoothly. Allow yourself to be awkward. You are stripping yourself."

I teach a Graduate Equivalence Degree class for people who want to get their high school diplomas after their class has already graduated. The whole purpose is to help them find their weak areas and to help them study so they can pass the exam. I take no grades, penalize for no absences. The whole success of the class depends on their own dedication, their passion for becoming educated.

When I explained all this the first night, five young people grinned at me, nodding vigorously. "Hey, neat," one young man said, "Why couldn't school always be like this?"

I smiled back, but I also said, "Self-discipline isn't for youngsters. The responsibility is in your laps—that's exciting, but also scarey. You can take the credit for your successes, but you also must accept the blame if you fail."

I guess I wasn't surprised when the next week only one out of the five came back. She brought two friends with her—she was dedicated, and passionate enough to spread the word.

Are you ready for this kind of intense writing, for a heightened devotional life? Journal writing is like active worship, the less timid you are at it, the more it will reward you. Spill out your hurts and fears right now, explore them, and then go searching the Scriptures and your heart even further. Do it with all your might.

Your Turn—Take one or more of these phrases and complete it:

"I really hate it when . . ."
"The most exhilarating thing that ever happened to me was . . ."
"I couldn't live with myself if . . ."

THE TABLET
OF SELF-EXPRESSION

*Let the beginning writer not ask him-
self then "How shall I write?" or "Who
shall publish it?" Let him rather say,
"What do I know of truth? What has happened to me and touched me so firmly
and finally that I will live with it always."*

Peggy Simson Curry,
Creating Fiction from Experience

The Case of the Disappearing Writer's Block

— I don't have anything to say.

— Please. It's been days since you wrote in me.

— (with a sigh) I must have writer's block!

— Poppycock! You're just lazy!

— How can you say that? I washed four loads of clothes today, put a stew in the crock pot, swept the floor, dressed and undressed Barbie four times and Ken twice and . . .

— Well, maybe not lazy, but not disciplined about writing either. I must not matter enough.

— You do matter. It's just that I feel all dried up inside, bleak. All the good ideas I used to have feel like the marshmallows I found in the cupboard last week— hard, unusable. If that's not writer's block, what is?

— Okay, I apologize. You do have writer's block, but don't talk about it like it's some kind of disease. It's not. It's fear.

— Fear? What am I afraid of?

— You're afraid of your own thoughts and you're afraid of not expressing them well.

— You mean, I don't want to write down what I'm really thinking or feeling so instead of dealing with that, I just give myself this gigantic block?

— That's about it. Pretty wimpy, isn't it?

— Why am I afraid of my thoughts or feelings?

— Maybe because they're embarrassing or spiteful or maybe even because they're sentimental.

— Yeh, you could be right. And I know I'm afraid of not writing well enough. That problem has strangled me for years, but I thought you had helped me overcome it.

— Journal writing *has* helped you. You're much less stilted and overly concerned with quality than you used to be. But I still see you pause and nibble your pen, trying to be clever. You don't have to be anything but yourself for me, you know. I love and accept you just the way you naturally are.

— Thank you, journal. So this problem is just in my head? I can't do anything about it?

— Sure it's all in your head, but it is a real problem and there's plenty of real solutions you can try to get rid of it:

1. Write about the block. Confront it, talk about it, meander all around the frustrations and the fears. Name them.

2. Write to the block. Have a dialogue with it to find out why it's there and why you want it to go away.

3. Write *exactly* what you're afraid to say. Face it, no matter how painful, silly or trite you think it is. God will give you the courage to face your sins— and your strengths.

4. Write from an altered point of view for awhile. Pretend you're someone else, like your cat or your neighbor or the wind whipping around the corner of your garage. If you're afraid, for a time, to be yourself, it may be restful to be someone else until courage returns.

5. Write what you feel on scraps of paper, and promise yourself you'll throw them away. This pact may release your emotions because you know no one, not your husband, not posterity, not even yourself, will ever have to read those words.

6. Write for a different audience than usual. Maybe, secretly, you're writing this journal for your mother

or for your husband or for your public when you're rich and famous. Maybe thinking about that audience is now freezing your mind. So write for someone else, someone uncritical and receptive, like your child or your best friend or your future self. Or write to God. Pour out all the grumblings and musings of the heart he knows so well. He will love you anyway, you can be sure.

7. Write as fast as you can for as long as you can. Don't reread, don't self-censor, just let it flow.

8. Make lists, anything that occurs to you, even if just shopping lists.

9. Relax before you write. Go running, exercise, take a shower or bath, or do deep breathing exercises, anything to get your body melding with your mind. You may notice that when you write with your body relaxed, the words don't matter so much, they just are, and the block has miraculously disappeared.

10. Try reading poetry or viewing art works. Let them stimulate your imagination until original thoughts start surfacing. Then grab any paper available and write.

11. Go some place new to write. Natalie Goldberg has a delightful chapter in her book, *Writing Down the Bones*, on writing in restaurants. She goes with a friend to some eatery during its off-hours. They sip coffee, scribble and read to each other whatever comes of their scribbling. If you can't do that because of children, write on your bed or in the bathtub. Try the backyard, climb a tree, any place that conjurs up new thoughts and sensations.

12. Change your clothes. Why not? Dress like an executive or a hobo or a clown. It may make you feel silly, but it may also release you from inhibitions you didn't even know you were feeling. It's hard to

write lady-like, careful prose if you're wearing your bathing suit.

13. My last piece of advice is a sure-fire block-breaker: "Do it anyway." That's what the pros do, even if they're sleepy, even if they're sick, even if they're blocked. Let the pages get filled. Later, you may even discover, they're not so bad after all.

— Thank you, journal. Already I feel more creative.
— Great! So what are you waiting for?

Your Turn—Almost everybody is blocked at some time. When you are, try some of the above ways to break through the block. After you've broken through, the next time you will be more confident that the block is conquerable; and the block, like an easily discouraged suitor, won't come calling nearly as often. To prepare for the next time you may be blocked, write down a list of topics you find difficult to write about, ones you avoid. Then, right away, force yourself to write two pages on one of them. See! You do not have to be enslaved by your fears!

Clustering: A Magic Tool

May my meditation be pleasing to him,
as I rejoice in the LORD.

Psalm 104:34

I discovered clustering six years ago when I was teaching junior high students creative writing. I had just read Gabriele Rico's book *Writing the Natural Way* and loved her concept so much that I'd done many of the exercises she suggested. Not only did the method enliven my writing and make me excited about what was hiding inside of me, but I was sure it could revolutionize the writing of my students.

Clustering is merely thinking on paper. It's not just doodling though, or list making, and it's certainly not outlining. I like to call it "tornado outlining," because it's chaotic and picks up bits and pieces and swirls them around in unpredictable ways. Here is a brief explanation of how to cluster.

Choose a topic, something you want to write about or something someone has *asked* you to write about (it can work as well for a school report as it can for journal writing). Pare the idea down to one or two words which you write and circle in the middle of a sheet of paper. Now all you do is let your mind wander, jotting down anything that occurs to you. Pretend you are on a psychiatrist's couch playing that association game. Write down anything and everything, drawing lines from the central word and circling each word or phrase as it radiates outward. Let the lines hook up with the last idea that inspired them.

For example, let's say your idea is "fear." Fear makes you think of darkness so you draw a line from fear and put the word "darkness" in a circle. Then darkness makes you think of your closet door when you were a child and how you hated it to be open an inch or two at night. So you draw a line from darkness and circle "closet" at the end of it. That makes you remember the white robe that peeked out at night and frightened you, which reminds you of your mother's wedding dress and how you didn't like it that she'd never try it on for you. This doesn't seem to be going anywhere, so you go back to fear in the middle again. You remember how afraid you were at a store once when you lost your father for a few moments, so you write "K-Mart." This recalls your father's face, a mixture of anger and relief when he found you, so you write down "Dad's fear." This makes you think of parents afraid to lose their children and the horror of the guilt that would haunt them forever.

Of course, you could go on and on. Clustering, however, has a purpose, namely, to release ideas, sensations, memories and connections that you may have never thought of without following the trail, so that you can write something important and powerful to you. It is a tool, not the end product. Therefore, eventually you must stop clustering and write. When?

You stop clustering when you feel the mind shift, when you know *this* detail excites you, this you *must* write about. It may even have little or nothing to do with your original concept. Unless you're doing an assignment, who cares? Go with what interests you because that's what you will write most powerfully. Perhaps in my web example I might end up writing about overprotective parents who don't trust their children to God's protection, and not about fear at all. If your subject calls you, follow.

Sometimes when you write you will use all or most of the details you dredged up in your clustering web. Sometimes you won't use anything but the last idea. That's fine. There is no wrong or right way to draw a web or to use it once it's drawn. In fact, being uptight about the drawing will ruin its effectiveness. The whole idea is to be open and responsive to whatever ideas come, to use some of the wonderful memories God has allowed to be stored in his most complex creation, your mind. I guarantee you will be thrilled with how it can magically transform your plodding, predictable writing into a journey of discovery.

Okay, so the idea worked great for me, but I wondered, "Will it work with kids?" Junior high students are about as open to innovation as most churches are to Christian rock. However, after they tried it, they amazed themselves and me.

Dull, cat-hat type poems became testaments to dead pets. A simple word like "fear" revealed sensitive stories about being friendless in a new town and quick ascents on basement stairs. I could see them touching reality at last, my secretive tribe who rarely admitted they liked anything, let alone class work.

Not all of them loved clustering. Extremely logical ones still preferred list-making and outlining, and the very shy and inhibited ones, who often liked to work at home on creative writing projects, hated it. I worked with a few of these individually, practically pulling out memories from their heads, and won some over, though one or two never converted. The ones who showed the most improvement in their writing were the students who had great imaginations but never knew it. They had been frightened and constricted by blank paper before. With this technique, they blossomed. White paper wasn't so scary—you just filled it up with this crazy clustering and, poof, you had an IDEA.

They grew to love exploring the twists and inklings of their minds like journeying down the Amazon, taking a jaunt into that lagoon or peering under those hanging vines. Then, when they found their treasure, they started scribbling. What a joy to see heads bent over desks, fingers gripping pencils with fervor, and the blessed quiet of concentration.

Sometimes we feel empty, like the windswept wasteland of New Mexico; but God put life there too, tiny plants and animals, blowing grasses, and people living just over the next rise under a tin roof that blinds the eyes of birds and scalds their feet. Clustering is a lazy looking for such things, instead of zooming by at 60 miles an hour. It's not purposeful and assertive charging ahead, but peaceful meandering, full of faith that what you may come upon has worth in some small way.

I have many journals that look like they were attacked by spiders because so many of the pages have these weird webs on them. But I will tell you, some of my favorite entries follow those webs. In them, I discovered jeweled fruits on grapevines, sweet and strange surprises that prove I am more imaginative than I thought. I have also used webs to help me figure out solutions to problems, plan events and write this book. It is a magical tool that can free us from thinking in the same old ways about the same old things. It can help us meditate on what the Lord has done in our lives, which is pleasing to him.

I believe God created our minds with such complexity because he wants to use our good ideas for his kingdom work. We must not use only the top soil, the easy stereotypic thinking. We must dig down. Discover the rich, black loam that is made up of all the leaves and lives and rotting of countless years. Bring it up and use it to grow lively writing.

Your Turn—Cluster around some word in your journal. Pick something with a lot of associations for you, like "joy" or "pain," or a color that you love, or the name of someone from your childhood, or a line that's said frequently around your house. Then, without thinking or planning, jot down everything that occurs to you, radiating out from the central word in one direction or ten. When you feel the mind-shift that says, "Yes, that's what I want to write about!" stop clustering and write. You may even discover things in this way that you need to pray about or talk over with others. Dig deep and see what happens.

Taming Your Monster Critic

For God did not give us a spirit of timidity....
2 Timothy 1:7

A peevish little monster lurks in my brain, peering over my shoulder every time I try to write, and mocking me, "You call *that* writing—pure drivel, if you ask me. Who do you think you are anyway, the next Hemingway? I wouldn't be caught dead pouring out all that stuff nobody cares about, but you just go ahead if you want to. Don't come crying to me if your descendents burn it in embarrassment."

As you can imagine, before I learned to tame this charming intruder, I didn't write much. What I did write often sounded stilted and overwritten. She simply drained me of my initiative, enthusiasm and, mostly, of confidence, which you need in abundance if your writing is to throb with honesty and personality.

If you too are having difficulty with your monster critic, let me explain why. We have two sides of our brain, the right side which is our creative, symbolic half and the left side which is detail-oriented and concrete. Much research has been done about left and right brain learning. Most of us tend to be predominantly one or the other, artists tending to be right-brained, accountants left-brained. The best learners, however, try to use and develop both sides of their brains because each serves important needs. We need our right-brain type of thinking for decorating a room, substituting an ingredient in a favorite recipe, or intuiting our way home when we're lost. However, we need our left brain when balancing our checkbooks, analyzing the logic of a politician or editing something we have written.

Most individual tasks require both sides. Let's say you're planning a party. You need to get some ideas about the theme, so you jot down a full page of notes. Your right brain is in her glory, pouring out all the chaotic and creative stuff that occurs to her. You could get your left brain into the act already now, but that wouldn't be very productive. *You need to have something to work with before you can critique it.* Once you've recorded all the ideas right brain has been offering you, then it's left brain's turn to look at this jumbled list coolly. She can weigh each idea according to cost, ease of execution, interest to you and your guests. She can cross out the bad ideas, put questions marks by some, and leave you with an edited list that should please you. You see, right brain and left brain can be an effective team—when we use them correctly.

The trick is in never inviting Ms. Left Brain, your monster critic, until you're ready for her skills. You must tell her in no uncertain terms to leave you alone. This journal is your private place, the place you pour out your honest feelings without censoring them because they're too silly or too long-winded or because your grammar ain't right.

Consider how your son would feel if he ran in after school breathlessly telling you about a home run he hit at recess, and you said, during a slight pause, "Don't say 'got no,' son." He might ignore you and keep going, but if you did it once or twice more, he'd probably give up and slouch away, thinking to himself, "She cares more about how I say stuff than what I say." The really sad thing is that if you had let him ramble on, even asking a few questions, he might have told you things he didn't even plan to, wonderful things such as how his coach's face looked and what his best friend said and the way the sky curved over his ball so slowly that his mind memorized it forever.

There is a time and place for everything. Your journal is not a place for editing yourself, for second guessing how you say things. Someday, you may want to go back over some entries and make them into poems or essays, and then you can let your monster critic out to prey on them. He's a whiz at helping you make sentences glow with tight and effective writing. However, he cannot blow life into lifeless writing ruined by his early presence.

I wonder sometimes if the devil uses our monster critics to keep us from writing anything with the power of truth. I used to suffer terribly from listening to my monster critic. I crumbled up ten times more sheets of paper than I saved, tearing myself up inside because I wasn't writing "literature"—whatever that means. This book you're reading would never have been written if I hadn't finally learned how to tame my monster critic.

So what if I'm not the next Henry James or Jane Austen? I'm God-loved and what I have to say is still important, *however* I say it. That's why my journals finally helped me get free from my need to write "perfectly." In them, I could muck around, write baby thoughts that never had to grow up into anything if I didn't want them to, scribble illegibly, and write fragments that would shock my seventh grade English teacher. In private, my journal could be like a child allowed to play in mud puddles. I knew if I had to clean her up for company I could, but meanwhile I let her create all the mud pies she wanted to.

I put this quote above my desk to look at whenever my monster critic starts to loom near: "No person—not even you—can possibly have any idea as to the worth of your story or book *until after it is written*" (Curry). It's like trying to frost a cake you never got around to baking. It's like nagging your children to keep the house clean for dinner guests when it's only 10 a.m. Sure, you can do it, but it probably won't work and will leave you frustrated besides!

This is what I learned to say to my monster critic when I began writing this book: "I'm just going to write down everything I can think of. No, it won't be organized or clever or beautifully rendered. I'll probably make lots of spelling errors and some logical blunders, but it's going to flow and be fun to write. It will contain the essence of me because I'll write fast and naturally. After I'm through it all once, you may then come calling. I will welcome you in fact. We'll sit down together with some tea and go over these words carefully, with high standards about organization and style and the final polishing. Maybe we'll even find out the writing isn't so bad after all."

When you keep your monster critic away, what will emerge in your writing is called "voice." Peter Elbow says in *Writing with Power* that "people often lack any voice at all in their writing because they stop so often in the act of writing a sentence and worry and change their minds about which words to use. They have none of the natural breath in their writing that they have in speaking. . . ." *How* do you ignore the critic, though? How do you find your writing voice?

Here are some tips: Write fast, write a lot, and follow your intuitions. If your words aren't you, you'll know later when you reread, and, if you want something for public viewing, you can cut that part out. You'll know you've found your voice, just like you know when you're in love. It's a rush of confidence, of joy, a sense of rightness. "Yes, that's what I wanted to say," you'll think, and your pen or keyboard will hardly be able to keep up with your tumbling thoughts. Maybe that's all inspiration is, finding your voice, finding what you have to say.

You must not plan what you're going to say. You really can't for one thing, because our minds are so complex and wonderful that they're always suggesting new avenues to explore that only just occurred to us. You might miss these exciting new paths because you don't want to "get off the subject." Remember this is not a paper for a professor—it is a place of discovery. Research scientists don't plan their results, they look for them, sometimes in most unlikely places. That's what you must do. C. Day Lewis describes it this way in *The Poetic Language:* "First, I do not sit down at my desk to put into verse something that is already clear in my mind. If it were clear in my mind, I should have no incentive or need to write about it. . . . We do not write in order to be understood; we write in order to understand."

I wish I could tell you that your monster critic will always stay away if you follow my advice. He still bothers me at times. I've found out, however, that the more I write, the weaker his whining voice gets. Soon, I'm so lost in pouring out what needs to be said that I can't hear him at all. "What? What were you saying? Something about this being truly fascinating stuff, I bet." And I wink as he slinks away.

Your Turn—Write a monologue to your monster critic. Tell him why you wish he'd let you write what you want to. Tell him how God longs for us to move in faith with confidence and energy, not always second-guessing ourselves. Pour out this dialogue very rapidly and do not allow yourself to reread it or erase or cross out any words. When it seems finished, then go back and change it to be better. This process should feel right because you're using each side of your brain for the tasks God fashioned them to do well.

L ists

A fun, but also illuminating, exercise to try in your journal: write down a list of the things that irritate you. This is what I wrote in my journal in November, 1985:

Things that Bug Me

1. People who think of everything in terms of how much it costs.
2. Waitresses who don't smile.
3. Men who ignore women and speak only to other men.
4. Dirty snow.
5. Mistreated books.
6. Old newspapers cluttering the house.
7. Leftovers I forget to use, and then they get moldy.
8. Baby socks that get lost in the wash.
9. Grown-up socks that get lost in the wash.
10. My husband complaining he never has two socks that match.
11. Unhung up clothes.
12. People who think that complaining is the only way to have a conversation.
13. Myself when I complain too much.
14. People who are too afraid or lazy to ask questions.
15. Husbands who won't ask directions.
16. Our faucet which takes an engineering degree to find cold and hot.
17. Washing diapers.

18. Kids who want to play piano beautifully but don't want to practice.
19. People who can't see the funny side of life.
20. People who won't talk about the serious side of life.
21. Myself when I pretend I'm not crying in a movie theater.
22. Running out of milk and bread.
23. Running out of money to pay for milk and bread.
24. Running out of gas to go and get milk and bread.
25. Myself when I laugh too much.
26. Myself when I never laugh.
27. The blankets that won't stay tucked in at the bottom of the bed.
28. Doing dishes after a big dinner.
29. Hair on the sink.
30. Crowded closets.
31. Kids who have to use the bathroom just when dinner is ready.
32. Kids who don't use common courtesy.
33. Myself when I forget to write thank you notes.
34. People who twist what you say to mean something else.
35. People who won't try new foods or places to visit or ways of doing things.
36. Our car.
37. What I do to my fingernails during a good movie.
38. Cracker crumbs on my freshly scrubbed kitchen floor.
39. Me when I forget to water my plants.
40. Brown, bedraggled, dying plants.

Notice how often what bugged me in other people also ended up bugging me in myself as well. Somehow writing out your irritations makes them seem not so bad, or at the very least, makes you consider how you might deal with them.

I've also done lists on "Things that Make Me Happy" and "People I Admire." It's easy. It's illuminating. And it's fun.

Your Turn—List at least ten things that—

—Irritate you.
—Make you sad.
—Make you happy.
—You'd take to a desert island.
—You'd give to your best friend if you could.

Divine Details

Indeed, the very hairs of your head are all numbered. Don't be afraid; you are worth more than many sparrows.
                                        Luke 12:7

If you've been writing regularly in your journal, by now you have pages and pages of memories stored. You have begun an heirloom your descendents may treasure more than Aunt May's snapshot library or Uncle Lester's home videos. I'm serious! Why? Because pictures don't catch the on-going details, the tiny habits, fleeting thoughts and bizarre connections that haunt our everyday lives. The best journals, on the other hand, abound with such trivia.

I don't think of it as trivia, however, and neither does God. Take a moment to browse through your Bible with an eye to discovering all of the details that burst from it. Because it's God's Word, full of the Big Idea of Salvation, we tend to think of it as high brow and inconcrete. Look, however: The Lord talks about hairs and sparrows and other mundane things. He names animals (Job 39) and plants (Isaiah 35) and eating utensils (Psalm 23) and cleaning procedures (Matthew 14). He tells stories about fig trees withering and women fixing dinner and a little boy's lunch offering. Details matter because in details we capture the meanings behind our actions.

Nabokov had this advice for young writers: "Caress the divine details." Don't just note them, caress them. Don't think of them as tiresome minutiae, but as divine—divine because God created everything unique.

Sometimes you may find yourself becoming bored with journal writing. You reread your words and they sound humdrum. If you check, you may discover you're generalizing. You're telling us you had a nice day or a terrible day instead of explaining about the swallows chirping in a nest in your drain pipe or about the gossip disheartening you at work. Pour out the details, the he-saids, she-saids, the gestures, colors, fragrances and textures. No, not everything, but everything significant.

Here's an example from my journals. Several years ago we took our two young daughters to their first wedding.

> Erin (age 3) kept calling the bride "Wendy" (her name was Cindy) and asking if she was married yet. Erin wore pink and looked like a baby princess. She kept hugging Daddy who seemed charmed by her excitement. Megan (age 5) sat on the aisle with her mouth open. Erin was frustrated that she couldn't see. They touched the bride's dress, lacy cream, when we went through the line. Cindy and Laura and the bridesmaid carried roses and candles. The church glowed with candles and candelabra everywhere. Megan cried and cried when it came time to drop them home so we could go to the reception.

How much of that would I have remembered from photographs? Very little, since we didn't take any! But that wedding, and our daughters' reactions to it, have been captured forever. I have word pictures in my journals of churches we've visited, vacation spots, and everyday mishaps and joys. I've tried to describe peculiar gestures and expressions of people I love and the arrangement of furniture in a room that seems like home. All of that is right there, in my journal, to enjoy and help me call up still more memories any time I want.

All those things deserve to be described specifically, and our reactions to them should also be noted specifically. As Natalie Goldberg warns, "Don't tell us about anger (or any of those big words like honesty, truth, hate, love, sorrow, life, justice, etc.); show us *what made you angry.*" To put it one more way, in the words of William Carlos Williams: "Give things the dignity of their names." Don't just jot down that you ate dinner at Grandma's. Tell us the cut of meat, what kind of potatoes she prepared, whether it was served on china or stoneware or plastic ware, and what exactly she said when the kids' boots tracked in mud (plus describe the expression that belied her words).

It takes time to build up reality piece by piece on paper, but your resulting journal will pulse with thereness and with your unique vision of your world. No, that's not egotistical. Remember, you and the way you see everything around you matter dearly, for "you are worth more than many sparrows."

Your Turn—Find an object from around your home that is fairly commonplace. Look at it closer than ever before. What is it shaped like? Describe the feel of it in your hands. Note the gradations of color, texture and line. If you dropped it, what sound would it make as it hit the floor? Smell it and try to capture its scent in words. If possible, lick it. Does it have a taste? Or, describe your favorite room in your home. Give as many details as you can, making sure you pick out ones that have the most significance for you.

R ichness

Let the word of Christ dwell in you
richly. . . . And whatever you do, whether
in word or deed, do it all in the name of
the Lord Jesus.

Colossians 3:16,17

What are the ingredients in your favorite recipe? If you're like me, your favorite recipes are also your richest ones. You know the kind—with lots of butter, cream, nuts, maybe a sprinkling from half of your spices—the kind that make you drive to the store just so you have that extra something they need. Rich journals, like rich desserts, don't just call for flour and water. We have to take that extra effort, and throw in lots of intriguing things.

By now, you've been keeping a journal for awhile. Pages and pages are there for you to reread. Aren't you proud of yourself? Take time now to reread them with this in mind: "How can I add more depth and richness to my Journal?"

More specifically, ask yourself:

1. Have I been searching "all things, even the deep things of God" (cf. 1 Corinthians 2:10), or have I been staying on the surface, relating how many loads of wash I did without explaining that I also yelled at my children and slammed the door on my way to choir practice?

2. Have I followed Henry James' advice: "Try to be one of those people on whom nothing is lost"? Anais Nin agreed with him when she said, "The

final lesson a writer learns is that everything can nourish the writer—the dictionary, a new word, a voyage, an encounter, a talk in the street, a book, a phrase heard. The writer is a computer set to receive and utilize all things."

3. Have I explored my spirit as it lives in Christ, recognizing that until my journal captures my inner life it will not be telling "the rest of the story"?

4. Have I been honest? Or do I try to make myself always the hero or heroine of my journal? I believe I wrote one of the most revealing passages I've ever put down on paper when I admitted to sometimes being the villain. With a three-month-old baby, I found myself struggling against the devil in a way I wouldn't have expected:

> The dark sister inside me—who is she? She's in me especially when I'm tired, tired beyond caring. My mind glazes over into some immoral realm where anything is possible, and nothing matters. Frightening. Fences go down. I think of what it would feel like to sit in this rocking chair at the top of the stairs and just let the baby roll out of my arms to tumble down the stairs. I almost can feel the muscles in my arms slackening, giving in to this idea. The struggle of reason. I tighten my hold, shakey with the wierd sense of having battled for possession of my will. Or when I long to fly off the road at 60 m.p.h. What would it feel like? The dark sister laughs at the idea that matter will stop me, hurt me. "You? You're invincible," she coos. "Have you ever crashed before at these amazing speeds? Faith in the road, don't you have

it? The road is everywhere and wide and glistening smooth under tires that fly over it like magic. You cannot die," she tells me. "Neither can your child."

"Lord, please help me fight her!"

5. Have I used my natural speaking voice in my journal, or is it stilted and proper? Do I use contractions and throw in jokes, slang expressions and fragments as I would in real conversations?

6. Have I explored various forms and moods or do I just keep relating the same basic experiences and thoughts in the same basic words?

Our journals have room for all kinds of experimentation: Try writing about your kids in Mother Goose rhymes, or give an account of your day in the King's English, or write a Greek myth about your family, or describe what you may have done if you'd been at Golgotha. I believe God smiles at a sense of humor and imagination, and that most of us err in the direction of uptightness rather than disrespect. I know that some of my zaniest, I-can't-think-of-what-to-write-so-I'll-just-try-this-dumb-idea entries are the ones I love rereading the most. They give my journals . . . richness!

Here's an example:

Me: Sometimes I think hard about you, and it sinks in: you're coming soon. Then I'll forget for awhile, and I get shocked all over. I'm going to have a baby!

Baby: I'm so shocking? Haven't you known about me for eight months

Me: Yes, but for most of that time you were easy to ignore. Even now you're mostly "the heartburn" or "this huge belly" or "the kicking."

Baby: Please don't ignore me! I'm here!

Me: I know I shouldn't. That's what scares me—my unpreparedness. I want the joy to be pure—not mixed with doubt, or worse, dazedness. I want to be immersed in the reality.

Baby: Reality is my sisters too, and they probably need you to ignore me now. Daddy might like a little attention as well. Later, you'll be all mine.

Me: Without resentment?

Baby: Nope. That's not reality.

Me: How come you're so wise?

Baby: I know you better than you know me. I feel your tensions and peacefulness, your hungers and your pains. I know how you breathe and sigh and cough. Do you know any of that about me?

Me: I don't know. Maybe some of it—maybe I could even pick you out of a hundred babies if I relaxed and let my body sense you.

Baby: Sometimes I worry too about coming out—if I'm ready, or if you'll want me.

Me: Oh, I want you. The excitement of welcoming you consumes me at times. I wonder how I can wait much longer. Please believe me! The clothes are washed, the bassinette is upstairs, the grandparents are planning to come. They called this morning, and we talked a lot about your arrival. It was fun to hear them so excited. We all wonder about your sex. That's the first thing I'll learn about you. Other people will probably tell me. But soon I'll be the one to discover what else you are. Come soon, baby. I do long for you.

Endnote:
Allison Danae was born six days later and weighed in at 6 lbs. 10 oz.

Your Turn—Choose a form or a "voice" you've never experimented with before. Then, tackling a subject that is important to you right now, talk about it in this very different way. It may well release thoughts and emotions about the subject you never faced before. Whatever results, the entry will be richer, more exotic, than a flour and water tribute to just another normal day.

Recapturing Awe

*"I tell you the truth, unless you change
and become like little children, you will
never enter the kingdom of heaven."*

Matthew 18:3

When I graduated from my teachers college, I thought I wanted most to teach junior high age children or even senior high. After a few babies and much substitute teaching at every level, I've since discovered who my favorite pupils really are: kindergartners and adults. You see, very young and the returning, mature learners have something in common—they want to learn. They can't help but learn, in fact, because they enjoy it so much. To them, school is always Saturday.

In lieu of teaching eager, awe-filled learners, I do the next thing. I write in my journal. In it, I can pretend to be any age, five or six, a baby in its crib, or even ninety-two. I can tell about the sidewalk in front of our house and how the ants walk across it like a battlefield, scurrying in desperation, carrying their dead comrades. I can tell about how it feels to lie with my cheek on sun-warm carpet, my sleepy eyes closed against the scalding brightness. Those aren't normal conversations among my women friends, but in my journal I can delight in these chances to see everything like a child again.

Dorothea Brande explains it this way in her captivating book, *Becoming a Writer:*

> The author of genius does keep till his last breath the spontaneity, the ready sensitiveness of a child, the "innocence of eye" that means so much to the painter,

the ability to respond freshly and quickly to new scenes, and to old scenes as though they were new: to see traits and characteristics as though each were new-minted from the hand of God.

John Gardner, an idealistic and inspiring teacher of writing, believes that reading should delight, that its first purpose should always be to delight. "To some extent, bad teaching is to blame," he says, "encouraging us to rise beyond and forget our most immediate, most childish pleasures—color in painting, melody in music, story in fiction—and learn to take pleasure in things more abstract and complex."

My journal helps me rediscover the simple pleasures that made childhood so vivid. For one thing, we can spend our whole lives examining the wonders of the natural world.

"'What's miraculous about a spider's web?' said Mrs. Arable. 'I don't see why you say a web is a miracle—it's just a web.' 'Ever try to spin one?' said Mr. Dorian" (*Charlotte's Web,* E. B. White). "The heavens declare the glory of God; the skies proclaim the work of his hands. Day after day they pour forth speech; night after night they display knowledge. There is no speech or language where their voice is not heard. Their voice goes out into all the earth, their words to the ends of the world" (Psalm 19:1-4).

We can also explore our own awesome relationship with the Lord:

As the deer pants for streams of water, so my soul pants for you, O God. My soul thirsts for God, for the living God. When can I go and meet with God? My tears have been my food day and night, while men say to me all day long. "Where is your God?" These things I remember as I pour out my soul: how I used to go with

> the multitude, leading the procession to
> the house of God, with shouts of joy and
> thanksgiving among the festive throng
> (Psalm 42:1-4).

Don't be afraid of your strong emotions. Don't be afraid to sound as awed and Spirit-filled as David.

Another idealist Judson Jerome said, "Science and art are but alternate paths to the threshhold of Awe." Our one true faith is, of course, the ultimate path to awe, but science and art can teach us much about our infinitely imaginative Lord: "Come and see what God has done, how awesome his works in man's behalf!" (Psalm 66:5).

One of the ways we can work at recapturing awe in our journals is by recalling the things we now accept on faith but that once confused us. "Who made God?" my second daughter asked as I tucked her in bed. "He just always was, Erin," I told her. She nodded solemnly, but her older sister, who was seven and trying to grasp the whole world, sighed deeply. "But, Mom, that's so hard to understand!" Try to remember how it felt to grasp such concepts. Explore your amazement in your journal.

Sometimes, when I get so embroiled in teaching doctrines to my children, I forget the mysteries of our faith. But it's the mysteries that fascinate the children. "One can't believe impossible things," Lewis Carroll's young heroine says. But the Queen answers, "I daresay you haven't had much practice. . . . When I was your age, I always did it for half an hour a day. Why, sometimes I've believed as many as six impossible things before breakfast."

Think of Mary. "For nothing is impossible with God," she hears from the angel, yet she must believe all this:

1. She is highly favored by God though she is just a young, humble girl.

2. She will have a child though she is a virgin.
3. This child will be the Son of God, the Messiah promised from David's line so long ago.
4. The conception will be performed by God.
5. Elizabeth, her relative who has been barren and is past child-bearing age, will also have a child.
6. All this is told to her by a messenger of the most High God—an angel!

Six impossible things before breakfast!

I hope I never get so busy, so grown-up, that I forget the wonder of my faith. I want to consider, like my daughter, Erin, what it really felt like to be Jonah in the big fish's belly, down there with "all those smelly fish." I want to ponder it all like Mary did so I can hang on to the awe, enjoying "the dearest, freshness, deep down things" (G. M. Hopkins).

Your Turn—Think of six impossible things that you believe. Consider them as you may have as a child. What would it feel like to be Moses, for instance, parting the Red Sea for the children of Israel? Or, look around you and ponder the miracles that stare at you, the baby who grows inside you, or the trees that throw their leaves down in fall only to grow new ones a few months later.

Remembering the Past

Prince, I warn you, under the rose,
Time is the thief you cannot banish.
These are my daughters, I suppose,
But where in the world did the children vanish?
        from *Ballad of Lost Objects*
                Phyllis McGinley

> *The palest ink is better than the most*
> *retentive memory.*
                Old Chinese Proverb

One of the best reasons to fill these pages with your words is that your memory can't be trusted. Things will slip away. Don't let your children, your friends, grow up or move away without tying them down on paper so you can *always* have a part of them. Journals are better than picture albums (and far better than shoe boxes full of unlabled snapshots!). In journal entries, you can hear snatches of conversations, smell again that exotic perfume, smile at a peculiar gesture your Uncle Dale makes with his hands when he's excited. Journals are fluid with change and flickering emotions, the he-saids, she-saids. If you've been honest, there should be few posed pictures, and no strained smiles.

For many months I kept a journal of letters written to my first two daughters. In one entry, I praised the value of remembering:

> I am reading Anne Morrow Lingberg's
> *Bring Me a Unicorn,* her diaries and letters
> from her youth. She reminds me of myself
> in many ways, thinking through the trivial
> into the philosophical (my husband calls

this "blowing things out of proportion"). She's introspective, a great reader, and a lover of writing. Yes, her writing. She inspires and humbles me—such a vocabulary, such a memory for quotes and details, such a wide education. She makes me wish I could go back and remember the feelings I had in my high school and college days with the same intensity. Why didn't I keep a diary all my life? How much further I might be now. I cannot come close to her ability to analyze her feelings and even more her gift of describing them as beautifully intermingled in atmosphere and conversations, with what stood on the mantlepiece and how the sun made the leaves shine.

Those things also used to move me more. I used to feel more sensitive, more alive to sights and smells. Why didn't I try to capture that aliveness? I could do it in retrospect—I may yet. But now it will always be an adult explaining a child. Gone forever is the child's explanation.

I suppose, daughters, you may guess where this is leading. Write now. Put it all down on paper in a special notebook, how you feel, what you do, and your impressions of who you meet and where you go. Don't wait to become a writer, an adult writer. It's a hobby, like tennis or swimming or chess, and you're never too young. You will discover things about yourself and maybe even polish a true talent. (It just struck me—is the Bible just a part of God's diary that he graciously gave us the key to? Inside, we find some wonderful secrets. Nice thought.)

Keeping a journal as my babies grew into toddlers and then into giggly, talkative girls, gave me a place to put down all the things they said and did that moved or amused me. Everybody's children say memorable things, but my kids are lucky enough to have a mom who writes everything down. One Christmas I even put in my letter a whole page of quotes that I had gleaned out of my journals. Maybe they will inspire you to write down what you can remember now and then to stay poised in years to come with your pen in hand.

Erin *(seeing trees blow):*
> "The wind's brushing the trees' hair."

Erin *(in the car one day, age 3):*
> "Mommy, did Daddy go, 'Eenie, meenie, minie, moe,' to pick you?"

Megan *(wearing a party hat on her forehead, age 5):*
> "Look. I'm a unicorn."

Erin: "That girl has bracelets on her teeth."

Erin *(sniffing a flower, age 3):*
> "I got the pink smell, Mommy."

Erin *(talking about Princess Diana):*
> "She lives in Kingland, doesn't she?"

Erin *(looking at me seven months pregnant):*
> "I forget what you look like skinny."

Erin *(at the hospital, seeing Briana for the first time, age 4):*
> "Mom, I thought you were just teasing about the baby."

Megan *(licking lines off of her animal-shaped vitamin, age 5):* "Now there's a monkey on my tongue."

Erin *(complaining about dandelions):*
> "I can't pick them anymore. They make my thumb taste yucky!"

Allison *(age 3):* "Mommy, are there Boy Cheese Sandwiches?" (as opposed to "Girl [Grilled] Cheese Sandwiches")

Allison *(age 4):* "Do burps live in our tummies?"

Megan *(after a long practice session at the piano, age 6):* "I can't wait until I can someday play piano in church and depress God."

A longer entry shows another memory I'm glad I captured on paper:

> Megan stood on the curb down by the stop sign to wait for Mrs. Zondag to pick her up for pre-school. I had a piano lesson, and the street is torn up in front of our house. Seeing her sit down on the cold sidewalk in her dress and tuck her knees up under it, reminded me of myself long ago. How I used to worry as I waited for people. Did they forget me? Is this the right spot? Did I come too late? I wonder if she thinks these things too. Her pink sweater flapped in the wind. The blue, hooded coat looked warm, but what about those bare legs? I seemed to say good-bye to myself as a little girl as the car finally drove up. Chilled, I hurried back into the house, feeling lonely.

When I reread my old journals, I'm often flabbergasted at how my memory has "altered" things. Facts have slipped away and in their place are inaccuracies and vague and incomplete shadows. I especially forget what else went on around the time of significant events, and this is where my journals really shine. They capture the whole fabric of my life, not just one isolated experience. So when I reread, I suddenly remember that the day the Challenger blew up was only a week after a woman was murdered at a convenience store two blocks from our house. At four in the morning, about the same time that I was nursing my baby in my safe rocking chair, she was gunned down the day before she planned to retire.

Also, barely a week and a half after the Challenger tragedy, a boy in a nearby town stabbed his mother and a neighbor lady to death near a Pizza Hut we often ate at, and, concurrently, we learned that one of our classmates from college had died from a blood clot and that the baby she carried was born with severe problems.

Is it any wonder that I brooded about death and such things for weeks afterward? I had forgotten, though, that all those things were so closely related in time, until I just reread it all in my journal.

I believe I forget partly because I'm always changing. "The past is a foreign country," a man once said. "They do things differently there." Because I change, because my moods, my situation, my interests, my goals, change, *I only remember what is significant to the new me.* But isn't that scarey? Have you known people who are adept at changing the past, forgetting dates and words said, and especially motivations and feelings? Irritating, aren't they? But I'm afraid I do it too, because when I reread my diaries, I see the way it first was, and how I've altered it in my mind. What I'm thankful for, however, is that I have my journals to reread. How else would I know what really happened, how I really felt? My journal keeps me honest, keeps me humble. It keeps me writing.

Your Turn—Write this promise to yourself in your journal. "I will try to capture significant events, important people, illuminating emotions in my journal. I will put down dates, the names of people and places, and sensory details that will surely leave my memory if unrecorded. I will prove love by cherishing daily what will soon change, by writing down the subtle characteristics of life as it seethes around me." Then begin to fulfill that promise by writing down the fabric of today in your journal.

Now the Eyes of My Eyes Are Opened

I Thank You God for Most This Amazing

i thank you God for most this amazing
day: for the leaping greenly spirits of trees
and a blue true dream of sky; and for everything which is natural which is infinite which
is yes
(i who have died am alive again today,
and this is the sun's birthday; this is the birth
day of life and of love and wings: and of the
gay great happening illimitable earth)

how should tasting touching hearing seeing
breathing any—lifted from the no
of all nothing—human merely being
doubt unimaginable you?

(now the ears of my ears awake and
now the eyes of my eyes are opened)

e.e.cummings

*Open my eyes that I may see wonderful things
in your law.*

Psalm 119:18

I imagine Lazarus may have said something very like that Cummings poem after he rose from the dead. Suddenly everything seemed brand new, the leaping trees, the "blue true dream of sky," and everything else he could taste, touch, hear, see, breathe. I've felt like that on days I wake up healthy after eons of headaches and fever. I look and really see what is around me. "Oh, God," I breathe, "how could I take all this for granted!"

Anne Morrow Lindbergh is one of my favorite authors. Actually, she's written little if you only count polished writing meant to be published. She wrote thousands of pages of journal entries, however, that thankfully have been published. She has the finest ability to see and feel with open expectancy that I have ever encountered. I love reading her descriptions of simple conversations or scenes, tinged with how a curtain moved in the breeze, or how a gesture spoke volumes about someone's sadness. She seemed to be observing everything with super sensitive antennae.

Yet, listen to what she expressed in one of her journals:

> This morning we drove to the field (air field); excited faces around of those who had already been up. I kept saying over and over to myself, "God, let me be conscious of it! Let me be conscious of what is happening, while it is happening. Let me realize it and feel it vividly. Let not the consciousness of the event (as happens so often) come to me tardily, so that I half miss the experience. Let me be conscious of it!"

I felt exactly that way when I was carrying my last baby. I wrote over and over in my journal about how I wanted to really sense everything while it was happening, somewhat because it might be the last time, but also because all my other births had happened so quickly that the look of the labor room, the nurses' names, the "scenes" couldn't be called up out of my memory because my inner eye hadn't been open. God must have heard my prayers, and he must also have a sense of humor.

With baby number four, my husband and I went into the hospital four times with false labor, each time staying an average of six hours. We played cribbage, sheepshead and solitaire. We talked at length to nurses, in fact got to know a crochety one so well that we hoped she would not be the one eventually to help bring our child into the world (she was). When visit five finally resulted in a baby girl after only forty-five minutes, I wasn't a bit disappointed. I had had my fill of vivid memories.

Being conscious of what is going on around us, being conscious in fact of what is going on inside us, is greatly helped by writing in our journals. If you have to explain what moved you or angered you, you will pay more attention while it is happening. You will keep the eyes of your eyes open, because you know if you don't, the journal will not be truthful. You know if you sleep while important things are happening to you, the journal will not be complete.

Christ in us gives us the desire for everything to be open and understood. His intensely revealing light wants to shine on every experience, every person, and show it for what it is. "But everything exposed by the light becomes visible, for it is light that makes everything visible. This is why it is said: 'Wake up, O sleeper, rise from the dead, and Christ will shine on you'" (Ephesians 5:13,14). When we rise from stupor, we can then witness, with eyes we rub in wonder, miracles all around us. Then we will say that, though you, God, are unimaginable, today I cannot doubt you—for the eyes of my eyes are finally open.

Your Turn—Today vow to be alive to everything. Write it all down. Tell how making dinner was an orchestration of sights, sounds, tastes and smells. Tell how your arms ached as you carried that child, but also how your cheek felt pressed against her hair. Tell about your conversations with God over that hard thing that happened. Drink it all in. Then spill it all back out on paper. The result will be a journal that shines with consciousness.

THE TABLET
OF LEARNING

*Nothing is more difficult than being
completely honest with yourself. . . . It
won't be easy. In fact, at first it will be
impossible . . . you've probably learned
to lie so well to yourself that you'll be
searching, not for truth, but for alibis. At
first you'll do a whitewash job to try
proving to yourself that you aren't really
a thoroughly despicable person at times.
But, as the months pass and you become
satisfied that Diary will keep your
thoughts securely locked in the iron box,
the truth may begin to shine through.*

Mel Ellis
"Afield with Ellis"
The Milwaukee Journal, 10/1/81

Do I Have a Book for You!

A good friend of mine wrote a book. It's a sprawling epic, spanning several generations, and so fascinatingly controversial it has critics hating and loving it internationally. I kept it on my nightstand for months, meaning to read it, wanting to, but never quite getting past a little skimming before bed. I felt bad. My friend could tell, too. Every time we were together I'd exude guilt: "I'll be getting to it soon," I'd tell him, eyes downcast. "It's all this substitute teaching I've doing lately, plus the kids have been sick. You understand, right?"

My friend nodded, but his eyes looked sad. I guess he wished I'd take the time because he had poured so much of himself into that book. In a way, it was he, and my rejection pierced through him like nails in his hands.

What if a prestigious magazine had asked me to review his book? Would I have gotten around to reading it then? You bet I would! I would have stayed up nights pouring over it, probably with a pencil in hand so I could scribble notes in the margins and mark significant passages. How I'd love talking about the book then with anyone who would listen, because I would have absorbed it into me. I also would get to know my friend through his book, better than I ever thought possible. Our friendship would blossom, and we would be communicating at last.

You probably saw this parable coming: Jesus is our best friend. Do we read his book? Does it sit on our nightstands where we stare at it guiltily each evening, or do we delve into it, longing to understand it, as a best friend should?

If you've been putting it off as I have in the past, then accept this as your assignment: Become a reviewer of God's word. Study it as if you had to communicate its message to thousands of eager listeners, hungry for its truths. It's now your job to understand it thoroughly, to write down your reactions, perceptions, not as a cool critic, but as a friend of the writer, a blood-bought friend, who will discover on every page the love poured out for you.

The will is a strange and stubborn creature. You may have to start writing your spiritual reviews against your will. God would love to have you to do it out of sheer joy and thankfulness, but sometimes we can't make ourselves feel enthusiasm for studying our Bibles. DO IT ANYWAY. That's the key to getting most things done that we put off, so why not use it to do something we know will reap us extraordinary benefits?

When I have been away from my Bible journal for a while, I return almost resentfully. I complain, I put off beginning, but then I finally sit down and open God's word and my notebook. Yes, this is my assignment as a Christian, I sigh. It doesn't take long, however, before—magic!—I'm into it again. I'm loving the words as they flower into meaning for me. I'm the Prodigal Son feasting at his father's table and wondering why I left in the first place. I'm Peter remembering my timidity around a campfire but now forgiven by the lakeshore. Why did I ever stray from Jesus' goodness? Why did I betray him with my distance?

The thrill is greatest however when I see that my friend has put me in his book. On almost every page I see that I am the character who needs comfort or forgiveness or encouragement. "How much he must have loved me," I marvel, "to include me in this great story, to make me in fact the focal point of the whole plot!" The reason he had come to earth was to save me from my sins, to rescue me from eternal separation from his love. Moreover, each reader will surely see herself or himself in the same way because my friend came for everyone alike.

Not only will I keep rereading this wonderful book now, but I'm moved to pass on my excitement to others. "Do I have a book for you," I say; and for the first time, people actually pay attention. Maybe it's because they can tell I really do seem to know the author.

Your Turn—Find a portion of Scripture you haven't read in a long time. Read it as if your best friend wrote it. Study it, mark it, and scribble in the margins. Then write in your journal about how much you learned about your best friend through this passage and what you learned about yourself.

The Examined Life

*Examine yourselves to see whether you
are in the faith; test yourselves. Do you
not realize that Christ Jesus is in you?*
2 Corinthians 13:5

*You hypocrite, first take the plank out of
your own eye, and then you will see clearly
to remove the speck from your brother's eye.*
Matthew 7:5

Whenever my husband Larry had a weekday free from
teaching grade school, we spent the noon hour with our
ham and whole wheat sandwiches and Perry Mason
reruns. We loved trying to guess who did it. After we found
out who, we loved seeing how the master lawyer got the
culprit to break down and confess. We'd watch how Perry
made him look deep into his own soul and admit the
blackness so obvious that it would soon be found out by
everybody anyway. Under vigorous examination, somehow he always made them confess, and we loved it.

Self-examination and confession are not fun, though
they can be fascinating. Part of me is drawn to books
and movies and people, the honest kind that ask hard
questions, that strip away my allusions about myself.
On the other hand, sometimes I recoil from such literature, entertainment and friendships, especially if they
ask me to change. I may be tired or ill, or maybe I'm just
afraid of change, so instead I read a light mystery or
watch a romantic comedy or make sure I find a yes-
person to talk to. After awhile, though, it's as if the Holy
Spirit whispers to me, "Okay, enough of this milk,
Ramona. Are you hungry for some meat again?"

85

Almost everyone likes to take self-inventory tests, like the ones in *Reader's Digest,* or the kind we took in high school to discover our vocational interests, our sharpened #2 pencils hovering over hundreds of empty circles. We like to examine ourselves, our likes or dislikes, our competencies and weaknesses—up to a point. However, I've never seen tests like these in any magazine:

—Test Your Non-commitment to Your Marriage Vow

—Identify the Commandment You Break the Most

—Rate your Self-righteousness Level

—Chart your Progress in Selfless Loving

Maybe such things are published somewhere, but I suspect the editors don't dream of riots at the magazine racks. That's not realistic. We'd rather rate our sex lives, our communication skills, our IQs, more than our spiritual health. It would be too scary to find out how far we haven't come.

Though I'm thirty-three years old, I wonder if I do still need the pure milk of God's word rather than the meat. When I look at the Christ-wrapped lives of other women I know, I feel ashamed. Whom have I led to Jesus' feet besides my own children? What acts of love have I performed outside of my own family? I have so much to learn, so much changing to do. It's time to take inventory.

If you, too, are ready to get serious about examining your life, you'll find your journal is an excellent place to identify the areas that need changing and to chart your progress. Also, you will find an able examiner in your Lord. Do you realize how often God used questions to draw out confessions, to make his children search their hearts? In the garden soon after the fall into sin, he called out to Adam and Eve, "Where are you?" (Genesis 3:9). And later to Eve he asked, "What is this you have done?" (3:13).

He asks the same questions of me: "Where are you?" and more damaging still, "What is this you have done?" Yes, Lord, I see my sins. I see I'm not always where I should be, in a peaceful, flower-fragrant walk with you, but rather in hiding, hoping you won't see my naked worry and my self-absorption. Forgive me. Yes, I've done many things wrong. Mainly, I've picked the forbidden fruit of distrust, continually taking myself out of your hands because I thought I knew better. No wonder I never seem to get far, I'm always struggling to catch up with where I think you want me to be, instead of raising my arms like a child and saying, "Please carry me there."

Jesus taught so often with questions, especially asking them of his followers. "You of little faith, why are you so afraid?" he asked his men in the storm-tossed fisherman's boat (Matthew 8:26). This question shakes me up, because I am often afraid. I'm afraid for my children's health and well-being. I'm afraid for food, clothing and that elusive thing called "security." I'm afraid of dying and of not having done anything important in the world's eyes before I go. Yet he whispers again to me, even as the gusty winds of problems quiet around me, "Why are you so afraid?" "I'm right with you," he implies. "Of course," I sigh happily, "how could I forget?"

If I'm having trouble believing in a hard doctrine like the Trinity or the Virgin Birth or the Resurrection, I try to visualize Jesus standing before his distressed disciples in the locked room, like a ghost, but with wounded hands that can be touched. He asks them (and me), "Why are you troubled, and why do doubts rise in your minds?" (Luke 24:38). I imagine their joy mixed with embarrassment, and I think, "How can I doubt he lives?"

When I'm lonely and sad, I need only remember the tender words he first said to Mary by the tomb: "Woman, why are you crying? Who is it you are looking for?" (John 20:15). Then I can search my heart and answer, "Because I need my Lord's love, yet he feels so far from me." Turning, I will at last know he is where he has always been, right next to me.

Or I can examine myself daily by listening to Jesus query Peter on the lakeshore: "Simon son of John, do you truly love me more than these?" (John 21:15) Three times Jesus had to ask that question, three times—once for each betrayal in the garden before the rooster crowed twice—so that he could erase the guilt and shame that made the strong man weep. I cry too, Jesus, when I think you don't know I love you, when my actions show more contempt for you than they do love. How can I show you I mean what I say?

> "Feed my lambs. . . . Take care of my
> sheep. . . . Feed my sheep."

> (John 21:15-17)

This has been a hard chapter to write. I'd like to show you only my wisdom and growth, not my sins, but what would that tell you about self-examination? How would that show you that journal writing can help you face your sins? More of the plank is probably in my eye, but I still urge you to work on your own speck. Examine your own life in your own journal and in your own heart. Don't be afraid of his questions. "My son, do not despise the LORD's discipline and do not resent his rebuke, because the LORD disciplines those he loves, as a father the son he delights in" (Proverbs 3:11,12).

A recent article in *Parents Magazine* was called "The Best Kept Secret about Discipline." The author says the secret is "example." He says that only when we live as we want our children to behave, will we influence them. If that's true, then that's probably how we can influence our unbelieving friends too—by leading loving, Christ-filled, joyous, trusting lives, and by taking time to be with them so they can see how we live. What a good reason to examine myself, then, so that the Lord

and I can make an example for others: "Feed my lambs.
... Take care of my sheep. . . . Feed my sheep."

Your Turn—Choose one or more of these questions to answer in your journal today:

1. Where are you?
2. What is this you have done?
3. Why are you so afraid?
4. Why are you so troubled and why do doubts arise in your mind?
5. Why are you crying?
6. Who (or what) is it you are looking for?
7. Do you truly love me (God)?
8. What kind of example do you long to be?

L ove Letters

Today God is still calling to his people,
Holding out His strong and loving hand.
Come unto me all you who are weary,
And I will lead you to the Promised Land.

Nancy Santiago
"Enter My Rest"

I needed a woman friend last year. When I prayed for one, God's answer came in the person of Nancy Santiago, who also, praise the Lord, turned out to be one of the most creative and inspiring women I've ever known. Nancy is a Jewish Christian whose burden for the salvation of her people has led her to compose and record Jewish-Christian albums.

As Nancy and I began to share a little of our hearts and lives, I was thrilled to find someone else who ignored her housework in favor of creative pursuits, someone who also hungered to talk about the deep down things. Not until I began to share my hopes for this book, however, did Nancy reveal something very private and important to her. She, too, kept a spiritual journal.

Somewhat different from mine, her journal is called "Love Letters." Each day, in a simple notebook, she wrote down a "letter" to God about anything that troubled her, confused her, or enlightened her. Then, after her letter, she wrote down an imagined response from her Lord.

How honored I was when she placed a sheaf of those "Love Letters" in my hands! I took them home and poured over them with mounting excitement. "I have to share these with other women," I kept saying over and over to myself. They glow with such honesty and a searching for deeper faith in her most-loved Messiah that they couldn't help but inspire others. I am thankful that, when I asked her, she graciously permitted me to share with you excerpts from her intimate epistles:

————————

— Dear Lord, hello. This morning has been so long and difficult. I've been aware of my loneliness when I don't spend time with you first thing in the morning. Such a lack of power in my life. My eyes look down instead of up, and it's not too long before I get dragged down into some "situation." I sense your presence, hear your Holy Spirit calling to me, reminding me that I haven't spent time with you yet. Thank you for your love, Lord. You truly go before me. Thank you, Holy Spirit, for being my wise and mighty counselor. Thank you that you're always there when I turn to you, Lord Yeshua [Jesus].
Forgive me, Father, for going into battle unprepared today. Thank you for the prayers of your saints. I love you so, Father. You are my mighty God, my counselor, my peace and my joy. You are my salvation.
Help me in all I do, Father, to look to you for all my needs. Help me to walk in your precious Spirit. I love you, my Lord. Father, I thank you and praise you for every relationship and every difficult situation in my life, as you are using them to teach me and give me practical experience in learning to trust you and follow you with all my heart. I love you.

— You're learning, my child. You're learning.

————————

— My Father, my God, my King. You are glorious and wise and wonderful, and, yes, I would taste of your love for there is nothing sweeter. I would walk in your love, Dear Father. You have given birth to me, and I owe you my life. Through the travail of your beautiful Son on the tree, you have brought me forth into the kingdom of God. And oh, what travail! Oh, my Yeshua, your blood flowed so freely for me. Will I ever know just what that means?

— It means eternal life, my child, and a seat at the banquet table of God almighty. It means refreshing for your soul and new vision and sight. It means the wine of the New Covenant. It means testing and seeing the Lord is good. It means blessing and life abundant. My child, I was more than happy to pour out my blood for you, for this lost, dying world. To bring joy brings me joy. Do not feel guilt over my death. It was meant to bring freedom from guilt. Take and satisfy your soul with all it means. My blood poured out means joy for you. It is what I purposed it should mean.

— Oh, Father, how do I integrate my daily life with the life of the Spirit? How do I stay in touch with you while making beds, cooking meals, washing dishes?

— My word, child. Speak my word to yourself for all situations. You have such a mighty sword at your side, yet you rarely use it. Take my word as a gift from me to you and use it in even the most mundane situations, and watch mundane situations turn into mighty fields of battle where great victories are won.

— My child, Do you not know yet that I love you? Come. Draw close to my heart. Whisper to me of your sadness. I will listen. There is no need to be dismayed when you have a friend such as me.

— I just don't feel I have anything to give anymore. Father, I feel as if I just need time alone to be *me*— not someone's mother or wife or friend or counselor, but just to be by myself for awhile and rediscover my relationship with you. I need a time of quiet feeding, Lord. Please help me.

— Every morning, child, you have that time available to you. If you will awaken early, get up, wash your face, then come to meet me for an hour, you will be fed beyond your wildest hopes and dreams. I will see to it that your well will never run dry.

Imagine that—an overflowing well, an ever present supply for my little lamb! Meet me, my child. No need for apologies, no need for explanations. I know your heart's desires. Come, my child, to a garden of delights.

Yes, and to a land of milk and honey. Isn't she wonderful? More to the point, isn't the Savior she writes about wonderful? To Nancy, because of her time in his presence, Jesus isn't some vague somebody—he's a person she is learning to know intimately.

Though this may embarrass her when she reads it, I must tell you that talking to Nancy is like going back two thousand years to a time when the disciples lived and breathed "the things of the Spirit." Everything she says and does reflects her mind-set. Could this be in part because her journal has helped her know Jesus, has helped her grow as his child, with a distinct "family resemblance"? I believe so.

Someday, perhaps, "Love Letters" will be published. Nancy's going over them now, at my urging, to see if she can fashion them into a book that can help other women in their walk of faith. That would be wonderful, but their primary goal has already been reached, namely, to teach, to mold Nancy Santiago into a woman with a peace that passes all understanding. "Where is this land where you may rest? In your heart when Yeshua is there."

Your Turn—Try to write some "Love Letters" to God. Pour out your greatest needs and desires, even when you're not sure what you mean: "We do not know what we ought to pray for, but the Spirit himself intercedes for us with groans that words cannot express" (Romans 8:26). Then search your heart, mind and God's revealed word for what he might say in answer to your inner groanings: "And he who searches our hearts knows the mind of the Spirit, because the Spirit intercedes for the saints in accordance with God's will" (Romans 8:27).

Music Lessons

*So what shall I do? I will pray with my
spirit, but I will also pray with my mind; I
will sing with my spirit, but I will also
sing with my mind.*

1 Corinthians 14:15

*Speak to one another with psalms,
hymns and spiritual songs. Sing and
make music in your heart to the Lord.*

Ephesians 5:19

A LESSON FROM A POEM

The girl had many bad habits. They prevented her
from playing the piano well and from enjoying her
music. She strained forward, peering at the music from
about five inches away, yet she assured me her glasses
didn't need changing. She stopped at every mistake and
replayed both wrong notes and correct notes over and
over, like a musical stutterer. Worst of all, she verbalized
her displeasure in herself continually: "I'm so stupid!"
"I know this, really!" "Oops!" It was pure torture to listen to her play.

As her piano teacher, I tried to lead her into confident playing, into a more relaxed, playful attitude
toward her music. I made her play a song repeatedly for
me until she could finally lean back, until she had few
mistakes and stopped lambasting herself.

"That's much better, Tania. Doesn't it feel like music
now?" I asked her, and she grinned at me. I jumped up
and picked out a poetry book from one of my book-
shelves. "Let me read this to you. It's talking about what
you just experienced."

A Lesson in Music

by Alastair Reid

Play the tune again: but this time
with more regard for the movement at the source of it
and less attention to time. Time falls
curiously in the course of it.

Play the tune again, not watching
your fingering, but forgetting, letting flow
the sound till it surrounds you. Do not count
or even think. Let go.

Play the tune again: but try to be
nobody, nothing, as though the pace
of the sound were your heart beating, as though
the music were your face.

Play the tune again. It should be easier
to think less every time of the notes, of the measure.
It is all an arrangement of silence. Be silent, and then
play it for pleasure.

Play the tune again: and this time, when it ends,
do not ask what I think. Feel what is happening
strangely in the room as the sound gloams over
you, me, everything.

Now,
play the tune again.

"You can't expect to get a piece in your fingers," I told her, "by playing it once or twice. And you surely can't get it in your heart and soul." She smiled and nodded, already leaning back a little on the bench. Then she played the tune again.

Writing every day does the same thing for me. I lean back more, the pen loose in my fingers, the words flowing with fewer jerky stops as I search for meaning. Best of all, I stop second-guessing myself: "Is this good?" "What a dumb thing to write!" "Oops!" Writing over and over, more words each day, gives me plenty of room to improve. So what if today everything is not totally honest or insightful or melodious? Tomorrow I will have another chance to play the tune again.

A LESSON FROM MYSELF

Sometimes I still play too mechanically and I concentrate too much. One late Saturday night I sat at the organ bench up near the rafters in a dark church. I wanted to go home, but the Bach prelude I'd decided to play in church the next morning wouldn't let me leave. It had a glitch in it, a hard phrase my mind and my fingers couldn't comprehend. Slowly, one note at a time, I tried playing it over and over. But this time the technique didn't work. Sure, I could do it in slow motion, but as soon as I tried working the phrase back into the piece at performance speed, disaster! My eyes would freeze on all those penciled-in fingerings and phrase markings and the notes jumbled together into a horribly tangled heap. My hands fell into my lap. I slammed the book closed. What was the use? Darkness waited around my little halo of organ light. "Will she leave?" it seemed to wonder.

I didn't leave. I put my hands back on the keys and forgot about them. "You don't need to look at the music. Feel it," I told myself. "Hear it. You've played it enough to have it down inside you somewhere. Let it come out." Peacefully, like a child playing in the sand, I let my fingers drift through the music. The phrase glided out perfectly! Not letting myself get excited, I did it again. Again, it came out whole.

A miracle! No, not quite, unless you consider God's design of our minds a miracle. I can get in God's way when I try too hard always to intellectualize things. Sometimes if we would just let our amazing subconscious do what it knows how to do, we could work wonders.

In my writing, too, sometimes I try too hard. I try to sound funny or smart or artsy. It shows. The writing is stilted and definitely not me, and sometimes it's even a heap of horribly tangled thoughts. Being playful in my journal is the answer—not caring so much if I get it right or not. When we least expect them, then, perfect phrases, like a joyful succession of harmonious notes, will glide out on the page and amaze us. Some people call this inspiration, but I believe it is simply getting my ego out of the way of my God-given talents. There is a time to learn mechanically, but there is also a time to let go and trust.

A LESSON FROM A LISTENER

I was feeling sorry for myself. "Nobody listens to my pre-service music or my postludes," I grumbled. When I was a new organist I remembered receiving several compliments and encouragements, but not anymore. I was just part of the worship woodwork, something to be taken for granted.

As I walked down the stairs from the organ loft, my fingers still tingled from the Paul Manz piece I'd played. It had been full of strange discordant chords that almost seemed to triumph over the deep bass melody of "Jesus Christ, My Sure Defense," yet not quite. I loved it. "Even if no one else did," I sighed self-pityingly.

To humble me, and perhaps to hearten me as well, Jesus sent a youthful woman of eighty to accost me in the narthex. "Thank you!" she exclaimed, her lined face beaming. "A piece like that reminds me that all of my sinfulness is the discord and Jesus is my resolution."

"I never thought of that," I told her, ashamed. I knew then I had a lot more to learn about my music and about my one avid listener. For whom was I playing? And for whom do I write—to be noticed by men or to glorify my Savior?

A LESSON FROM A STUDENT

For eight years I'd used a traditional saying to help my piano students learn the treble clef line notes:

"Every Good Boy Does Fine." I'd learned it from my piano teacher who probably learned it from hers. It smacks of the flavor of McGuffy Readers and wood-stoves and an apple for the teacher.

Last month I learned a new saying from a blonde boy with mischievous eyes: "Empty Garbage Before Dad Flips." Since it makes me laugh, I use this one now. An old tradition has passed away. The moral? Don't be afraid to change the way you do things, the way you write, the way you talk, the messages you give your children. And don't be afraid to use humor. It's an amazing mnemonic tool. In this last month, *every* beginning student I have, knew his or her treble clef line notes perfectly!

A LESSON FROM A MOTHER

Learning to play the piano takes great patience. So does teaching it. That first year of teaching I'd sit beside my students and writhe in frustration. How I longed to toss aside their hesitant fingers and play it for them. "See how nice it can sound," I wanted to say from between clenched teeth.

Gradually, year by year, I grew more patient. I can now say the same hints and reminders three times in an afternoon and not mind. I can listen to jerky scales and *know* that, with a few fingerings changed, next week they will flow much better. There seems to be a rhythm in my repetitions that feels right, and I find pleasure in knowing that, if I explain this concept in just this way, young eyes will light up in understanding. I know because it has worked before. It will probably work again. Patience, after all, is often simply knowing what will work.

One first-grade girl I taught for a year was a typical student, maybe even better than most. But her mother, an ex-teacher at home raising four children, didn't believe me when I assured her that Theresa (not her real name) was doing "just fine." She wanted Theresa to be progressing much faster. She wanted Theresa to be practicing much more. She wanted a lot more from Theresa than I did.

At one lesson, Theresa told me that her mother and she bickered constantly over practicing. So I talked to the mother. I told her that in first grade many things are new and overwhelmingly difficult. My goals for Theresa were for her to enjoy music, to learn her notes well, and to share her songs with her friends and family. That's all. There would be plenty of time for hours of dedicated practice, but right now, "let's just give her the idea that music is great fun!" "But she's not where she should be by now!" the mother complained bitterly. "On the contrary, she's exactly where most children her age are," I insisted gently. I thought I got my point across.

One week later, however, Theresa's mother showed up at my door. "Theresa won't be taking lessons anymore," she said with tears in her voice.

"Oh, no! Why?"

"I'm afraid we got into a big argument about her practicing, and . . . " she paused in anguish. "I ripped her piano book up."

She looked right at me, her eyes begging me to understand. I was amazed at her honesty.

"Well," I said carefully, "we could get her a new book."

"Don't you see? That won't help. Until she and I can work this out, it's just causing too much friction. I can't take it. Maybe later."

She left, and I sat down to think. Why would a smart woman, a Christian mother, and an excellent former teacher put so much pressure on her first-born daughter and on herself? Why couldn't she just be more patient?

I believe that patience is gained through knowledge, as well as through prayerful searching for it. My own first-born daughter is taking piano lessons now—from me. She too is in first grade. She doesn't practice as often as I would like, but that's where I have an advantage over Theresa's mom. I *know* how much she practices in comparison to how much my other students practice. She is typical, perhaps even better. Even at the piano, as I move her fingers to the right keys, I am usually at ease with her. I know how fast she will learn, which things may come hard, which concepts may take months or years to sink in. Sadly, I think, "If only Theresa and her mother could be more patient."

The moral? Have patience with yourself as a journal writer and as a follower of God's word—not complacency—patience. You should always be moving forward, learning and trying new ways of writing and living and loving—moving forward slowly, sometimes, and by leaps and bounds at other times. If you don't have patience, you may be tempted to give up. "I can't write!" you'll say and throw the pen down. "I can't live like Christ—why do I even try?"

Yes, you can write. You can live like Christ when he is the one doing the living through you. Remember that it is a process, a journey, one that requires great patience and daily dedication.

A fan once said to the great pianist Paderewsky, "I'd give my life to be able to play like you do."

Do you know what the genius answered? "I did."

Your Turn—You have areas of your life where you are especially knowledgeable or skilled. Think of how those areas might teach you about your writing or about your spiritual life. Explore lessons you may have learned about patience or tenacity or proficiency or productivity. Sometimes we forget how many parables Jesus used from real life to teach us about the spiritual realm.

Writing Down Your Dreams

In the first year of Belshazzar king of Babylon, Daniel had a dream, and visions passed through his mind as he was lying on his bed. He wrote down the substance of his dream.

Daniel 7:1

In my dream, someone ushered me into a long white room where several people lay on low tables or cots. All were legless or blind or ugly with deformities. They may as well have been aliens, for I was repulsed. The person showing me through this room explained that these people were "The Guides," the most respected people in their society. When near puberty, each child in this region was assigned a Guide to help him or her gain wisdom on the road to adulthood.

"Guides?" I scoffed. "They can't even walk."

"Exactly," my companion agreed, "and that is what helps them to see beyond the merely physical world. Let me introduce you to one."

The man I met was stunted, with shriveled legs and arms. He lay flat on his back and stared at me with tiny, deep-searching eyes. He had a voice like melody and harmony together, and he told me he would be my seer.

"But I'm not a child!" I bristled.

"Are you not?"

I wish I could record for you how I made the transition from doubt to trust, but that part of the dream has faded. I only know that I did. Eventually, what my guide said, and how he said it, inspired me to trust him and travel by his directions.

Strange as it may seem, I believe that dream meant something important. I believe God can use even our dreams to help us, if he so desires. He may warn us about wrongdoing that threatens to distance us from him. He may warn us about our own pride or to preserve our soul from the result of unrepentant pride. Or he may even warn us about physical dangers.

Perhaps my guide dream was a warning against my pride. Maybe God wanted me to stop intellectualizing my faith so much, to start reaching out in a more child-like acceptance of his ability to guide my life. Until I believe so simply, his guidance would be as ineffectual as a handicapped midget's. He cannot force me to go where he directs. I must listen carefully to his gentle voice and then step out in faith.

The dream taught me that lesson. Some may say the devil could have also put this dream in my night. True, but I have tested what I learned according to God's Word, and it seems in accordance. Like Thomas, I could continue to smirk and demand further proof, but instead I will trust that as a child of God, even my dreams can be used for my good.

Some dreams will not be so important, but they may still reveal fascinating aspects of our personalities. They may help us put a label on vague fears or dilemmas. They may show us an answer or a creative option to a problem we're experiencing. Our dreams can do none of those things, however, unless we remember them!

A journal provides a place to record your dreams. It is a very popular use for journals right now. My guide dream would never have been able to influence me if I hadn't written about it in my journal. Bits and pieces might remain, but not as much as you have heard, and what the memory can't hold can't be used effectively.

Of course we have to be careful not to put more trust in our dreams than in our heavenly Father or in his word. As the Lord said to Jeremiah:

> I have heard what the prophets say
> who prophesy lies in my name. They say,

"I had a dream! I had a dream!" How long will this continue in the hearts of these lying prophets, who prophesy the delusions of their own minds? . . . Let the prophet who has a dream tell his dream, but let the one who has my word speak it faithfully (Jeremiah 23:25,26,28).

We must remember the vast difference in reliability between the visions of our own minds and the inspired Scriptures. Dreams can intrigue us with their hint of mystery. God, of course, is infinitely more mysterious, and he created the mind and the subconscious. Keeping all that in mind, we can nonetheless enjoy learning from the third of our existence we spend in sleep.

To record your dreams, simply keep your journal near your bed. Whenever a vivid dream happens, as soon as you wake up, capture it on paper. If you don't do it right away, or at the very latest before nightfall, it will slip away forever. In the middle of writing this chapter, I took time to reread some of my old journals. I hoped to find one or two other dreams in them that would be examples of dreams captured on paper.

What I found surprised me! I didn't find one or two dreams in those volumes. I found over ten—ten dreams I had completely forgotten about, but, when I reread them, flowered in my memory like huge exotic plants. Yes, I murmured, there's the dream where I tried to buy a doll in an antique grocery store for someone who needed one desperately. There's the dream where my husband and I were being held captive on a monastery campus with smiling guards and no fences. If I hadn't bothered to write down those dreams, they would have been lost. Already, they were lost to my conscious memory. Only by rereading them in my journals have they again become part of my living memory. Again I can use them to better understand my subconscious fears, obsessions and needs.

We need not record every dream. But once in awhile one passes behind our eyes, a deep dream that haunts us, one that shimmers with meaning. Write that one down and keep it. God may have something to teach you from your vision in the night.

Your Turn—Put your journal beside your bed for a few nights. Resolve to scribble words about the half-formed images or full-length dreams that come to you. Sometimes just the decision to record them makes the dreams come. Also record what you think the dreams may mean, or why you may have dreamed them, or even what God may be saying to you with these visions.

THE TABLET
OF LIVING

The significance of man is not what he attains, but rather in what he longs to attain.

E.B. White
Stuart Little

Slowing Down

Be still, and know that I am God.
Psalm 46:10

Picture yourself eating a runny ice cream cone in 90 degree weather. You're licking as fast as you can, but your hands and arms are getting streaked with vanilla. Faster, faster, catch that drip, now swirl around to the other side. Never mind enjoying it—this is survival! You against that ice cream cone, and you're determined to win. I wonder, however, did it ever occur to you to refuse to fight, to walk back to the drive-in counter and ask for a cup and a spoon?

"But that's not the game," you shrug. "It's supposed to be a battle, me against the ice cream cone and the merciless sun." But do you taste the ice cream? Does it melt in luscious dollops on your tongue or slip down unsavored, like jello or Pepto-Bismal?

Here's the parallel for our lives: Do we play the busyness game, the traditional battle of fragmentation and rush, rush, rush, being all things to our church, our family, our employer, our friends and our community, even when it doesn't reward us with much peace or enjoyment? Or do we say, "Stop! I give in. Time to slow down. Where's that cup and spoon?"

Three years ago I made this frazzled entry in my journal:

> I have so little time to notice anything but what must be done to feed us, clothe us, or keep up our appearances or responsibilities. I want to notice things again, like what kind of day it is, the really important things in other people's lives. I'm so sepa-

rate. I can't even be a witness to my faith because I rush around so much that I don't feel compassion for anyone except my own family. I like to think it will get better soon, when my girls are all in school. But will it? I see many women twice my age frantic with this same sense of hurry that I feel: "There's too much to do and not enough me to go around."

Is this trusting in my Savior? I must find peaceful days, less need to be everything for everyone, time for long, aimless walks, for meditating on God's Word, and for reading and talking to my daughters without soon sighing, "Sorry, Honey, Mommy has work to do." I must pray for the strength and wisdom to know how to spend the precious gift of time my God has given me.

Soon after that journal entry, I decided that this need for a daily time of meditative aloneness wasn't an option. It was necessity. If I didn't get it, I became tense and unhappy. When I slowed down and took time for myself in this special way, peace crept back in, and, miraculously, I could also care about others more deeply. Anne Morrow Lindbergh says in *Gift from the Sea* that women especially spill out to others without taking the time to fill back up their own reservoirs. A quiet time with my Bible, my journal, my prayers and thoughts fills me up so that, amazingly, I have the patience and even the joy to keep going.

Untangling ourselves so we can have this filling-up time can be difficult. Your family and friends, accustomed to having you "available" for every minor crisis or burdensome task, may resent the time you begin to reserve for yourself. They may also become entranced, however, at the new you. The new you savors conversations, instead of absentmindedly fretting about your long list of "must-do's." The new you shares insights from Scripture about everyday needs. The new you, because you have gazed honestly into your sinful soul and repented before God daily, bubbles over with a newfound compassion and love for others.

Schedules can be good, and goals wonderful, but shouldn't they *serve* the real you, the person God intended you to be, instead of enslaving you in the bondage of hurry? Life isn't a contest to see how much you can accomplish. It isn't a rat race. That's what Jesus saved us from in the first place with his death, the eternal striving to be good enough. Just because you have the most commitments, the most people dependent on you, doesn't mean you are the most "spiritual."

A favorite poem of mine helps me remember the joy in slowing down:

I Meant To Do My Work Today
by Richard Le Gallienne

I meant to do my work today,
But a brown bird sang in the apple-tree.
And a butterfly flitted across the field,
And all the leaves were calling me.

And then wind went sighing over the land,
Tossing the grasses to and fro.
And a rainbow held out its shining hand—
So what could I do but laugh and go?

Go back and get that cup and spoon. Take action that will make your wishes come true. Stop and taste the ice cream.

Your Turn—Describe a part of your life that seems out of control, that threatens to enslave you instead of enrich you. Tell your journal why you feel the way you do. The next chapter should help you find solutions, but right now you must identify the problem.

You Have All the Time You Need

Pretend you have walked into a Seminar on Time Management. Maybe this time, you think, I'll find out how to control my life, how to rise above my guilt. You sit down in the front row, gazing at the spokeswoman as if she's an oracle. "Save me," you implore her with your eyes.

"Hello, everybody," she says, "I am here as an imposter. Though the brochure said I would show you how to manage your time, I can't do that. I don't know how."

Audible sighs and grumbling seethe all around you. Who is this woman? How dare she pull this stunt?

"Please, ladies, You may stone me if you wish, but let me explain first."

Her face is so sweet and comical that there is faint laughter. Yes, you'll give her a few moments. After all, the babysitter has been hired; you can smell lunch cooking in a far-away kitchen. Sure, you'll listen, but you slump down in disappointment.

"In fact," she continues, "if you walk out of here dissatisfied, you may pick up your check for this workshop as you leave. I believe, however, you will not walk out. I believe when I've finished, you will thank me with tears in your eyes.

"You see, ladies, I invited you here because you are exactly as I was six months ago: selfless, driven, and unhappy worrymongers. I know, because why else would you take such a workshop?"

By this time, you're nodding and sitting up straighter. "Yes, that *is* why I came. That's me. Why won't you tell me how to change?"

"Also, I know you have the capability to change. Change, notice I said, not become more efficient. You see, being efficient is not all that difficult. Women do it all the time. They make lists, roll up their sleeves, and do the job. You are intelligent women, you could do that too. You could have the house, the life, of your mistaken dreams—IF YOU REALLY WANTED IT."

"But I do want it," you think. "Don't I?"

"I don't think you do want it. Not badly enough. You divide yourself between housework, your job, your children, your spouse, and your own self-nurturing until you feel as if you're going crazy. It's all compromises. *Nothing* is done well. You're the Jill of all trades and proficient at none. Peace is as illusive as a clean floor, crumbs and grease marring it daily, and until you can completely eradicate all this, you feel you cannot be happy."

"Yes," you murmur. "That's exactly how it feels. Isn't it sad?"

"I offer you peace, ladies. Listen to me—peace! Do you want *that* badly enough? I think that's what you sought here today. It's what I wanted out of Time Management: peace like a huge featherbed I could sink down in and know that someone else would make in the morning.

"No, I'm not a maid service. I give you better than that. My friend and Savior gives you better than that. Jesus once said to his disciples, who also lived busy, stressful lives, 'Do not worry about your life, what you will eat or drink; or about your body, what you will wear. Is not life more important than food, and the body more important than clothes?' (Matthew 6:25). He might have added, if he were speaking here today, 'and a peaceful home more important than a perfectly clean and organized one?' He went on to explain what our priorities should be: 'Seek first his kingdom and his righteousness, and all these things will be given to you as well. Therefore do not worry about tomorrow, for tomorrow will worry about itself' (Matthew 6:33,34).

"Jesus hates to see his followers worry. Isn't that amazing? I sometimes think you can tell which women are the pillars of their churches by how much they worry. They worry about the altar cloths fraying, about the coffee pot draining improperly, about the young people putting the chairs back incorrectly. To hear them fret, you would think the gospel proclamation depended desperately on a church running as smoothly as a socialite's estate. Yet, our Lord walked into the hills to teach people and never even brought along provisions. Of course, he could feed them with a miracle, but the people themselves did not *expect* this. They simply trusted that those things that weren't so important would somehow take care of themselves

"I believe that when God said over and over in Genesis, Exodus, the Psalms, the New Testament, 'Don't worry. Trust in me,' that he meant it. Didn't he calm bustling, worried Martha with the words, 'Mary has chosen what is better'? (Luke 10:42) He can calm you too, friends. He can help you to choose the better way to spend your time.

"I am not telling you to be lazy and irresponsible, to use my words today as an excuse to watch soap operas all day and dress your children in pinned together rags. I *am* telling you to deepen, to become honest about seeking the truly important things to you. I am telling you to push aside silly guilt feelings about wrinkled sheets and bathtub rings and concentrate on love and creativity."

Creativity? What a strange word to hear at a workshop on Time Management, but maybe not so strange at an Anti-Time Management workshop.

"I believe that creating and love are almost synonyms. Creating is *loving God's world,* seeing it, being in the present, absorbing all you can. You yearn to express this love, so you create a painting, a story, a song, a happening, an idea."

As she talks her eyes glow, but you're beginning to doubt again. "All that may be true," you think, "but I'm not creative. This new way of managing life can't be for me after all."

"But we create so seldom," she goes on. "Why? Because we think creativity is for geniuses, the gifted ones. No, it isn't! Push that idea from you now. God created each one of you with a unique mind and with the ability to imagine, to combine ideas, words and materials with limitless creativity. Creativity is a word we've made too big and awesome. It doesn't just mean inventing great works of literature or pictures to hang in the Louvre. It also means thinking of a clever theme for your choir concert, making a Halloween costume, designing a poster for VBS, writing your thoughts down in a journal, or directing a neighborhood Christmas skit. It's these small gifts of love that can enrich your days, give them joy and meaning, that can be the means for you to reach out to others through your unique talents."

Timidly, you raise your hand. She pounces on you like a leopard. "A question?"

"Does that mean I have to let my house go to shambles while I sit scribbling away at the kitchen counter?"

"Young woman, you don't *have* to do anything. Jesus asks you to love him out of the fullness of your thankful heart. That's also why you love others and why you create—in joyful thankfulness for life eternal. If your messy house impedes your joy and your family's sense of peace, then clean it. But don't clean it like a martyr, scrubbing up microscopic germs you peer at until your eyes ache. Do this too out of love and only as much as necessary. Save yourself for the things that are better: studying God's words, acting in love and creating. The standards each of you set will differ. Be sure, however, that you set a standard for you, and not to please your finicky friend or your mother's hovering spirit. Why are we so afraid of our houses? How can they be more perfect than we are?

"I will give you *one* piece of advice. Start now to throw out everything that has no impact on your life:

clothes you rarely wear, old magazines, memorabilia that have lost their significance, worn out furniture you hate to look at. It sets you marvelously free, and greatly reduces clutter."

Another woman raises her hand. You have started something. "What about my job, my need to chauffeur Jennifer to her activities, my two Bible studies, choir, Ladies Guild, the PTA and . . ."

"I see. Yes, you are busy. Do you like that feeling?"

"No, not really, but those things are good, aren't they?"

"Do you also have time for idle walks, daydreaming, prayer, study, and long intimate conversations with your husband or a woman friend?"

"You must be kidding!"

"Then you must disentangle yourself from some of your activities. Jesus found time for walks, prayer, and long, intimate talks with his disciples and strangers. Can we do less than follow his example?

"The creative urge in us is strong, but it needs quietness to flourish. You need quiet moments to explore your thoughts, ideas, problems and solutions. That means no radio, no T.V., no busywork, unless it frees your mind. You must learn to live fully in each moment, cherishing it, even when you are alone. At first, you may feel restless with meditative silence. Gradually, however, it will become an oasis you return to joyfully.

"It's time for you to end your frantic, stressed-out busyness, to go home and change. It's time to start saying 'no' politely but firmly to things others could do just as well as you. It's time to take on projects only when they seem to be God's will and involve something you will tackle passionately and creatively. There is no time for empty busyness. There is time to leave whole hours open for projects that glorify God and allow you to pour in the uniqueness of your personality and vision. There is time for playing games with your children, for telling jokes, for hiking a trail all by yourself. There is never enough time in the world for everything others think you should do, but there is plenty of time for all the things you long to do.

"From today on, every time you worry, hand your worry to Jesus. Tell him, 'Please, Lord, take this bad habit of worrying from me. Let me enjoy each moment as a gift from you, not straining towards the future, but content to rest in your buoyant arms right now. Fill me with your peace and wisdom so that I use my time to have ideas and to create what can shine out in a world full of darkness. Help me trust daily that my very moments are in your hands.' "

You are entranced by her words, but you have one more practical question.

"I want to believe I can change, but what if my family won't let me? What if they complain: 'Where are the chocolate chip cookies?' 'Why can't we watch T.V.?' and 'How come you aren't like other moms?'"

"At first, they'll hardly notice you have changed. You'll notice. You'll be able to feel your own heart beating in your throat; you'll hear birds singing that never seemed to be around before; but all that is intensely personal. After a few weeks, however, they'll start to notice. 'Hey,' they'll say, 'Mom's different lately. She's not yelling so much, and she smiles a lot. She even let us go barefoot in the back yard, and she came out and went barefoot too!' Do you really think they'll miss those cookies or the T.V. shows? And what's wrong with not being like those other stressed-out moms who haven't learned our secret?

"You see, what happens when you slow down and enjoy each day is that you begin to release resentment. Remember how often you resented your children's noise and interruptions when you had your long, joyless list of "Jobs To Do." Try tearing up those lists. So what if company is coming? Take your preparation time for thinking up ideas for conversation. What have you always wanted to know about these people? How did they meet? What makes them sad? How has the Lord moved in their lives? Leave the floor—will they really look at it? Do only the love tasks for them—making a pleasant (though not show-offy) meal, perhaps arranging a lovely table. Then rest so you can enjoy their presence. Maybe then your children won't say, 'Stay out of Mom's way—company's coming!'

"Do you know what else I don't resent? Death. It's true! I used to be very afraid of death—even as a Christian. 'I have so much to do, to be,' I wailed at the Spectre of Earthly Finality. 'Please, Lord, don't let me die before my last girl is eighteen or before I publish my first book or before I've evangelized my non-Christian friends.' But now that I am peacefully creative every day, now that I see life as a process instead of a destination, it doesn't matter that I have not accomplished what I have dreamed. Tomorrow I could die, and yet today, since I live moment by moment for Jesus, I will have accomplished my goals: trusting in him, loving others and pouring myself into creative work I use to glorify him. Of course, I still have long range goals. I want to write more books, see my children to adulthood; but that is in God's hands. Today I will simply take the small steps up the mountain and enjoy the scenery as I go."

You leave the workshop a new woman. You roll the car windows down as you drive and scarcely care that the wind blows out your curls. You reach for the radio dial and then change your mind. "Today," you decide, "today, I will listen for my own heartbeat and the quiet, timeless movement of my thoughts." And in each moment you feel God's presence and the wonder of forever. You have all the time you need.

Your Turn—Write a prayer in your journal asking the God of time and eternity to help you focus on the "things that are better." Name those things. What do you really long to spend your time doing? Then do them. Trust that he will take care of you today and tomorrow, even without your fretting.

Travel Tips

*Love must be sincere. Hate what is evil;
cling to what is good. Be devoted to one
another in brotherly love. Honor one
another above yourselves. Never be lacking
in zeal, but keep your spiritual fervor, serv-
ing the Lord. Be joyful in hope, patient in
affliction, faithful in prayer. Share with
God's people who are in need. Practice
hospitality.*

Romans 12:9-13

Everybody's always telling you what you should do: slow down, enjoy life, set priorities, become more spiritual and loving. Few people, however, tell you how to go about doing these things. What are the steps? The steps you need to take to reach your goals will be different than the ones I take, but if I tell you what mine are at least you'll see how most of us get up the mountain, one small step at a time.

I've changed many of my habits and activities in the last few months. I've become less stressed, more at peace. I've decided to write this book and have *accomplished* it. I've had Christ permeate my life through daily Bible study, journal writing and prayer. All this didn't happen overnight though. It took thinking about what daily things I had to change, the small movements, words and attitudes. It took writing down those small steps.

My husband and I have always loved to travel. Even though we haven't been able to walk along the moors of England or kiss the Blarney stone, we have managed to transverse the U.S. enough to develop our own travel tips. We believe that traveling is an art that can be done well or poorly, and if it's done poorly you squander never-to-be-recaptured chances at wonderful memories.

Here's what we've learned:

1. Travel light. Never take more than you absolutely need and won't mind repacking in less space.

2. Travel with a sense of wonder. Expect to experience serendipidity at any time, an overgrown path you follow to a spectacular view, a tiny cafe with the best food in seven states, a stranger who knew your parents when they were young.

3. Travel positively. Admit there will be inconveniences, bad food, lumpy beds, surly residents, but see them as real-life experiences that will perhaps teach you more about the people and locality than any swank hotel possibly could

4. Travel with humility. Do not be constantly comparing your city, your home, your way of life to this new environment to prove how much better yours is. Instead, always see its strengths and what you can learn from these people and their ways.

5. Travel courteously. When you are courteous to those around you, not only will they probably respond in kind, but you will spread an atmosphere of graciousness.

6. Travel gratefully. Thank those who in many little ways make your journey more comfortable and enriched.

7. Travel with an inquisitive mind. Ask questions constantly. Think of this journey as a course you've been longing to take. Learn words in the language and customs of the region. Soak in all you can of these people and this place you may never see again.

8. Travel with patience. Do not expect everyone to be quick to accommodate you, to change for you. You must respect their time and fit into their lives, not force them to adjust to your needs.

9. Travel as if everyone you meet is your brother or sister, as if you have one thing in common with everyone: God as your heavenly Father through Christ.

The other day as I was reading Romans 12:9-21 the passage somehow reminded me of our travel tips. If you take a moment to reread the tips, perhaps you'll see how they can apply to your walk of faith, how they do somewhat resemble the Bible passage above. What common threads do you notice?

Both give high regard to the forms of love like hospitality, devotion, harmony, patience, courtesy, gratefulness, humility. Politeness has been called "love in little things." Politeness takes time, though. If you want to be polite, you stay around and chat. You look into your host's eyes when he talks and follow him when he wants to show you his artifacts. You expect to be amused and charmed by his words. You live and speak the language of caring.

If instead you're always rushing around taking snapshots for when you get home, you won't see beyond the end of your camera lens. If you try to do all things for all people, you become a blurred, indistinct every-person. Getting to know people takes time, and loving them requires definite and even painstaking effort.

When I became serious about slowing down my life and learning how to travel through it more meaningfully, I made myself a tape. On this tape I recorded my own voice reading my travel tips, worded positively. Then once a day, usually as I washed the dishes, I would listen to this tape. I would hear my own voice telling me about the person I longed to become in Jesus (the person, in fact, because of his redemptive blood, that I *already was*). It reminds me daily of the tiny steps I need to take to reach my goals. Here is the script of my tape:

"I am at peace.

"I am filled with the Holy Spirit's calming balm.

"I do not seethe with ambition and strife. My soul lies restfully within me, content to let the Lord guide my moments and days and to give me the fruit of my labors as he sees fit.

"I rise early so my day starts in control.

"I do not rush around, but calmly attend to each necessary task, taking time to smile, to laugh, to share moments with other people.

"I prepare for each day the night before, making sure my priorities are in order. I write myself notes on all important matters, so my memory is not taxed with non-essentials.

"I tell no lies to make things easier for me. I know that peace springs from a clear conscience.

"I do not procrastinate. I do important tasks right away, so my mind is free to dwell on people and ideas, not duties.

"I keep my home relatively neat and orderly so that I can pass tranquilly through my surroundings, at ease with them.

"I remind myself daily, however, that people come first, not houses.

"I leave early for all appointments and wait patiently with a book or my journal in hand, seeing those waiting moments as free gifts of time.

"I plan ahead for all contingencies and then leave worry in God's hands, for "in all things God works for the good of those who love him" (Romans 8:28).

"I keep an open mind about standards and preferences, allowing for others' points of view and giving into theirs when love constrains me.

"I count my blessings daily, realizing how God has given me riches beyond belief in my husband, my children, my health, my talents and my circumstances.

"I ask questions whenever I'm unsure of directions or instructions. I will not waste my time or any other person's because of my own timidity or pride.

"I can say 'no' politely but firmly to people who want to sap my energy and time for projects that I feel God has not led me to take on.

"I take time for myself, for prayer, for meditation, for daydreaming, for reading and writing, or for just soaking in a bathtub. I know that, before I can pour out to others, I must also fill up my own reservoir with spiritual refreshment.

"I keep everything simple, my surroundings, my clothing, my meals, my life, so that clutter and wasted moments do not drain me.

"I stop and rethink my goals often and schedule each week so that I'm using my time as I and the Lord really want me to.

"I befriend non-worriers, relaxed people who value long talks and impulsive happenings. You can't meet butterflies if you never sit by cocoons.

"I sleep well every night and rest when I'm tired.

"I am at peace. It flows through me like a wide and gentle river. May the peace of the Lord be with me always."

These are my hows, my steps. When you have discovered yours, then begin your journey. Go forth in faith, like a world traveler, but also with the open, eager eyes of a baby.

Your Turn—Choose what kind of a traveler you want to be under God. Then consider the daily steps, the attitudes, the actions, you must take in order to be such a traveler. Write in your journal a script like mine where you describe yourself already doing those things. If you have the courage, record it on tape and listen to it often. Gradually, you will begin to be the person God has called you to be, step by improving step.

The Maybe Mommy

Who of you by worrying can add a single hour to his life?

Matthew 6:27

"I am the Maybe Mommy. So when my begging daughter asked, 'Can I go on a walk around the block with Stephanie?' I said the inevitable: 'Maybe.' But she is only five and I meant maybe after lunch, a nap, a trip downtown to buy kindergarten shoes, maybe after the nuclear holocaust.

"Her little sister always hugs my maybes to her chest with trusting, pudgy hands, stroking them like precious promises that will soon grow up to be true, but this firstborn child just stared at my maybe, then ran crying into her room. What is a Maybe Mommy to do?

"Later always seems nicer for decisions. Later, worry might release it's tight hold on my chest and leave my voice free to shout Yes. Later, the cards might reshuffle and deal us a rainstorm or an emergency, anything that will make No inevitable and easy to say.

"I will not admit my maybes are lies. They are simply lazy no's or scaredy-cat no's or sometimes a yes with so many ifs trailing after it that her walk will not be glorious tripping anymore, only plodding responsibility. Yes, you may go, if you stay on the sidewalk, if you kick no rocks, talk to no strangers, and if you return in seven minutes and twenty-three seconds. Often my maybes are time-strangled: maybe when you're seven or twenty-one or a grandmother in a wheelchair— maybe when you go to heaven.

"I am the Maybe Mommy, too afraid to open up Now so it's big enough for the both of us. Too afraid of Yes.

Too afraid of No. But also afraid of all my maybes. What does she think about, I wonder, all alone in her afternoon room? Maybe she whispers into her soft, wet pillow, 'Maybe, Mommy, maybe I won't always love you.'"

I wrote those words in one of my journals about four years ago. I wrote them during a time of hard transition, when I was not as comfortable being the firm adult because it hadn't seemed so long ago when I myself was the child. I was tired of being wishy-washy and yet not quite ready to give a firm no or a trusting yes. I wasn't ready to trust my parenting instincts, nor to trust my God with my daughter's safety.

This problem I had as a mother reminds me of a Mother Goose rhyme:

> "Mother, may I go out to swim?"
> "Yes, my darling daughter. Hang your clothes
> on a hickory limb, but don't go near the water."

What we hand them with love, the hand of fear steals back. Fears strangle joy. But how will our children ever grow up healthy and whole without our hovering? Care is not worry, and until we face our worries, our care will seem only like worry to them.

I've written countless times in my journals about my worries. It seems to be a sin I, with the Lord's help, have to do battle against regularly. In my entries I've described the sin of worrying about money, the sin of worrying about my children dying (usually due to some terrible neglect of mine), and the sin of worrying about the effect of my worrying. By confronting these worries, though, I believe their impact is lessened. In fact, it's almost as if, in the act of writing them down, I give them to Jesus to carry for me.

Afterwards, I don't dwell on them anymore. I don't wonder over and over if I did the right thing by not letting Megan walk with Stephanie. I also learn from them what I may do differently next time. Next time I would take that walk with my five-year-old and her older friend. Together we would enjoy that sidewalk journey without fear and without risk, and maybe Mommy would even discover the world is not such a scary place after all with Jesus by her little girl's side.

Your Turn—Make a list of your pet worries. Tell about the ones that nag you at midnight and about the silly ones you hate to admit. Then, one by one, give those worries to Jesus in prayer. Ask him to help you conquer them, either by finding solutions that minimize their power over you or simply by forgetting them.

How to Big Talk

Always be ready to give an answer to the hope you have in you.

1 Peter 3:15 (Beck)

Small talk irritates me. Often it flows out of my mouth in nonsensical rivulets that I can't seem to stop. I fill time with it, kill time with it, until I can escape to the people I really want to be with, where I can at last discuss the subjects I really want to talk about.

What is my small talk?

Snobbishness? Perhaps I think the people I inflict my meaningless chatter on won't understand real truth. I limit them.

Laziness? Or is it that it's so much easier to fill silences with weather talk, humorous complaining, gibberish about baseball scores and new dresses.

Boredom? With others—or with myself?

A Lack of Love? I know if I only engage in small talk, I won't have to exert myself to find out who my listeners are, what interests them, or discover who I am in relation to them. I don't care enough to discover their uniqueness.

What, on the other hand, is big talk? You know what it is. It's staying up until three o'clock in the morning with a sister trying to understand why the church seems to have failed her. It's the argument in the dormitory over creation versus evolution. It's clasped hands at a funeral. It's being "ready to give an answer to the hope you have in you."

Unfortunately, in my life I've indulged in far too much small talk and not enough big talk. Don't get me wrong—small talk has its uses. We have to employ small talk in the early stages of most relationships so we won't scare people away. It's the rare spirit who will accept our heart language immediately, probably because most listeners need evidence that we will also listen and accept their own heart language. Most of us, however, err on the side of talking trivialities for too long rather than on the side of scaring off people.

How many friendships have never developed because I couldn't go beyond small talk? How many people may have taught me and touched my life dramatically if only I'd bothered to know them more intimately? I have wasted too many moments, too many opportunities for ripening friendship, because my mouth and my mind were stuck on automatic pilot.

In one of the journals I kept in high school, I wrote about a moving sermon I heard based on this simple text: "The disciples were called Christians first at Antioch" (Acts 11:26). Why were they dubbed with the name of Christ? Because, the young vicar explained, everywhere they went the holy name of Christ was on their lips. What began as a name of derision became a symbol of their continual habit of speaking about the one who loved and died for all men. Am I worthy of the name "Christian"? Is Christ's name on my lips so often that I can be branded as one of his followers?

The disciples big talked! That doesn't mean they never gossiped about the prices in the market place or compared last week's fish catch with this week's, but they also did not waste opportunities to speak of things enduring. I, too, want to use such opportunities. I want to bubble over with sincere, friendly, yet meaningful conversation.

To help myself with this goal, I started writing in my journal ideas about how I could improve my conversations, how I could become adept at natural-sounding big talk. Here's what I came up with:

1. Explore the facts of someone else's personality and history. Think of several questions I wish I could ask that person. Then find a quiet moment with him or her and ask one.

2. Memorize these six verses and mention them when anyone seems interested in what my faith is all about:

    Matthew 5:48, "Be perfect, therefore, as your heavenly Father is perfect."

    Romans 3:23, "For all have sinned and fall short of the glory of God."

    Romans 6:23, "For the wages of sin is death, but the gift of God is eternal life in Christ Jesus our Lord."

    John 3:16, "God so loved the world that he gave his one and only Son, that whoever believes in him shall not perish but have eternal life."

    John 3:36, "Whoever believes in the Son has eternal life."

    Ephesians 2:8,9, "It is by grace you have been saved, through faith—and this not from yourselves, it is the gift of God—not by works, so that no one can boast."

3. Remember 2 Timothy 1:7 when I feel shy, "God did not give us a spirit of timidity, but a spirit of power, of love and of self-discipline."

4. Drudge up stories from my life about answered prayers, witnessed miracles, God's power in changing me, sins forgiven, fears laid to rest, problems still being worked on with God. Write them down in my Bible or a notebook and then share them with others! Don't be afraid to show weaknesses—"for my power is made perfect in weakness" 2 Corinthians 12:9.

5. Don't become humorless and preachy. Trust in God to work the miracle of faith or understanding without my vehemence. Remember what a good

story-teller Jesus was and how often he let his listeners figure out on their own the moral to the story. Even light-hearted joking has its place in a relationship, just like dessert has its place in a meal. It shouldn't be the whole meal, but it can leave a nice taste in the mouth!

6. Don't be afraid to listen more and talk less. Pick up on sighs and averted glances, read faces and gestures. See hurt and loneliness and bitterness and boredom. Then mention them.

Yes, I may be rebuked for being nosy, but that's far better than never reaching out to help a human being. I may even be surprised how welcome big talk is to others. Sometimes, to people who are hurting, the whole world seems to jabber on and on about the weather.

Your Turn—Use the six steps I devised, or your own, to improve your ability to big talk. Becoming a person who cares more about what others have to say than about what we want to say is part of this lesson. Practice these love conversations on paper, then move beyond your journal by practicing them on people hungry for a friend.

Joy in Discomfort

But we have this treasure in jars of clay to show that this all-surpassing power is from God and not from us. We are hard pressed on every side, but not crushed; perplexed, but not in despair; persecuted, but not abandoned; struck down, but not destroyed. . . . Therefore we do not lose heart. Though outwardly we are wasting away, yet inwardly we are being renewed day by day. For our light and momentary troubles are achieving for us an eternal glory that far outweighs them all. So we fix our eyes not on what is seen, but on what is unseen. For what is seen is temporary, but what is unseen is eternal.

2 Corinthians 4:7-9, 16-18

One of my main themes is joy in spite of everything. *I don't think that I am pollyannish; my characters suffer, they die. They experience pain, alienation, frustration—all the hardships of life that real people experience. But, my heroes and heroines, the characters with whom I most identify and who are most important to me, all insist on joy in spite of everything.*

Tom Robbins
Writer's Digest, February, 1988.

THINGS THAT GIVE ME JOY

1. Kissing my daughters on the cheek as they sleep (though I wonder, "Did they brush their teeth?"

and "How long has it been since I bathed them?").
Joy in spite of worry.

2. Listening to a quartet of young Christian musicians in concert (though the church's air conditioning has broken down in 85 degree weather and my daughters, having guzzled diet pop at Burger King earlier, make eight individual trips to the bathroom between them). Joy in spite of perspiration and embarrassment.

3. Eating out (though it is a luxury we can ill afford). Joy in spite of guilt.

4. Reading a thrilling mystery or a magical fantasy late into the night (though the pillow never supports my head just right and my arm keeps falling asleep and the light doesn't illuminate the page evenly and in the morning I'm dead tired). Joy in spite of discomfort.

5. Talking to people about spiritual journals (though some people laugh at the idea, saying they don't have time, and how in the world could they write anything worthwhile, and why don't I just keep my nice little hobby to myself). Joy in spite of opposition.

When I was young, I thought, "If I can just finish college and get married, everything will be perfect." Later, I decided that if we could just get even financially, then perfect happiness would be ours. Deep down I knew my happiness really rested in WHO was in control in my life, not in my circumstances, but I still liked to play that little wistful game of "What if? . . ."

Sorry to have to tell you this, friends, but the perfect marriage, the perfect house, the perfect job, is absolutely impossible. No matter how much you love each other, or how much money you have, or how talented and disciplined you are, there will still be arguments and strife, there will be leaky faucets and mismatched wall paper, there will be drudgery and unfair promotions and unappreciation. Translation: Get real.

Getting real means realizing that your contentment and joy must rest on something outside of your circumstances or it is much too vulnerable. If it doesn't, think of everything that can wreck it: disease, calamity, betrayal, boredom. That's where the world differs markedly from the children of God. To people who do not have God's Spirit working in them, striving after perfection is a way of life. "I can have it. I must have it, "—it being the ultimate high, the eternally sensual relationship, amazing riches, power or maybe just constant validation. How sad, isn't it? They'll never be able to have what they must.

Thank you, Lord, that you have shown me the path to true joy. "You will fill me with joy in your presence" (Psalm 16:11). That means that no matter if I'm feeling sick or depressed, no matter if my beds aren't made or the children always mannerly, I can still be joyful; for you, Lord, are with me, you are loving me and uplifting me no matter what my circumstances or my sins, "for I have learned to be content whatever the circumstances" (Philippians 4:11).

I used to believe that if all Christians could just get together on some hill somewhere, join hands and sing, it would be glorious (something like that great scene at the end of *How the Grinch Stole Christmas*—remember?). Perfection, right? Now, after a few years of church work and child-rearing, I know differently. Inevitably, problems would arise. There'd be people with sweaty palms and others who'd refuse to touch them. There'd be a tenor singing off key and three other tenors trying to switch places to avoid him. There'd be altos upset because their part was so boring and basses and sopranos who never got around to memorizing the words. There'd be kids tired of standing so long and a few put-out people who'd refuse to sing at all because their favorite song wasn't picked. Am I right?

Life is full of irritations. We can choose to dwell on them, of course, like the Real Princess (she's that girl who couldn't ignore a tiny pea under zillions of mattresses), or we can develop thick skins that withstand minor irritations admirably. It helps to understand that God allows us to experience problems for a reason: he develops tough-skinned Christians, their faith strengthened and fired by adversity. If we bruise or get discouraged easily, how effective can we be? Our moaning and groaning not only wastes time, but it sends a powerful message to others: "If Jesus can't even lift her above the little things that go wrong, how can he help me with my completely messed up life?"

The old saying is true—"When the going gets tough, the tough get going." The tough ones, who can keep their eyes on Jesus and the joy he brings no matter what happens, become the mountain-movers, the ones who will amaze and lead people with their peace, their idealism and their steady dependability when everyone else is falling apart or getting fanatical or becoming morose.

Your journal can help you practice joy in discomfort. Every time something irritates you, especially if you know it's unchangeable or trivial, write out your frustration on paper. Also pray on paper for God to help you rise above your pettiness, sweetening your attitude and granting you the wisdom to know what should be ignored or, if possible, changed.

Sometimes complaining is simply a bad habit, a conversation technique. It's tempting to fake camaraderie by whining together about the pastor or the boss or your favorite institution. If that's your bad habit, work on it immediately. Nothing can breed dissatisfaction faster than constant complaining. Remember what God says our thoughts and speech should be:

> Whatever is true, whatever is noble, whatever is right, whatever is pure, whatever is lovely, whatever is admirable—if anything is excellent or praiseworthy—

think about such things. Whatever you have learned or received or heard from me, or seen in me—put it into practice. And the God of peace will be with you (Philippians 4:8,9).

Another way to use your journal to help you achieve joy in spite of everything is to list your joys, the true and deep ones, and do it often so you can see how they are changing and you are growing. Here's my list recently reworded:

THINGS THAT GIVE ME TRUE JOY

1. Knowing that my daughters rest in God's all protecting arms each night.
2. Talent in young people that is being used to proclaim their central joy in Jesus.
3. God's assurance that he will take care of us all, feed us, clothe us, shelter us, no matter what may come.
4. Books of all kinds that teach me the ways of man and the ways of God.
5. The Lord's promise that he will reap the harvest, working faith and understanding in hearts perhaps made softer because I spoke of Jesus.

Those are true treasures in the clay jars of our everyday lives.

Your Turn—Make a list in your journal of the things, simple and profound, that give you joy. Keep a page or two blank after this list so you can add to it from time to time. Read it over when the irritations and set-backs of life threaten to keep you focused on the seen rather than on the unseen. Thank God for the things on your list and ask him daily to help you claim "joy in spite of everything."

The Touch of Death

*I am the resurrection and the life. He
who believes in me will live, even though
he dies; and whoever lives and believes in
me will never die. Do you believe this?*

John 11:25,26

Darkness nibbles at my toes. For the first time, death
has touched my intimate circle—real death. Not the
kind that haunts other people's dreams, that snatches
away their loved ones. That death is a distant cousin to
this death that has invaded our family, or so it seems to
me. How was I immune to this pain for so long? Why,
Lord, did you wait all these years to visit me with the
indisputable fact of my mortality?

Where is my father? Just last month I got a letter,
another epistle about sewer problems and such. He
told about having to carry buckets and buckets of water
up the basement stairs because the plumber couldn't
get there till after the weekend. Of course he didn't let
Mom help, and not just because she's the one with the
heart problem, but because she's a woman and
shouldn't have to do such things. He'd also sent along a
mind puzzle for me to enjoy and use with the kids I
teach. "He's always thinking up ways to amuse and
teach me after all these years," I remember thinking.

Now I look up at the stars and wonder if they smile
and groan at his jokes. Where is he? Where is this heaven
he inhabits, which I believe in but can't comprehend?
Death is so weird, so obvious, and yet so unbelievable. As
we all watched that casket go into the ground, I felt
almost nothing. That isn't my father in there. It's just
some mannequin dressed up in Dad's new suit (bought

only last month). I'd made myself touch his cheek—that soft, talcum-smelling skin, crinkled from years of smiling—and I shuddered at the plastic feel of it. That's not something God-made anymore; it's chemicals and funeral-parlor artistry. It is not my dad! When he left, he must have taken the essence of his body with him. It's like a puppet now, without a hand inside, a popsicle sucked dry, a kite without some wind.

My mind understands this, but my heart yearns to talk to him again. I wish I could share musings, jokes and intellectual puzzles. He loved God's created world so much and was intensely curious. Are you exploring paradise right now, Dad, binoculars in hand?

I've been telling people about his death. "Did you know he was only sixty, that he wasn't a pound overweight and that he played racquet ball twice a week?" They pale. Their eyes glance down, as if they don't want to hear any more. Of course we don't want to hear it. We want to believe, despite people falling like flies all around us, that we will be the exception. We will not die, at least not soon, not surely until age eighty or until we have lived richly and accomplished many glorious things for God.

I keep telling them, even when they don't want to hear, because we must admit our days are numbered. We must begin to look at each day differently, hold our children more tenderly, teach them more diligently about God's ways. We must treat our spouses and our friends as if tomorrow they may pass beyond. We must reach out to people we don't know as if we have very little time left to make a difference. So I'm using you, Dad, I hope you don't mind. I'm using you to keep me soft and waiting. When I eat, food sticks in my throat. My eyes feel large and luminous, as if something is whispering to me repeatedly, "Look, pay attention. This too is passing."

Each day of course I speak of it to fewer people. I stop feeling like I'm waiting for something else to happen. The quietness, the attentiveness, fades. That's good too or I would never start laughing or working again, as you, Lord, would have me do. But I also hope I never totally forget again. I hope I remember that all this is temporary, and that what is essential is invisible to the eye. I refuse to wait any longer, therefore, to seek first the important things, to speak of my Father's plans to others, to be his witness who is only passing through this world.

Dad, wherever your heaven is, you're on God's missions now full-time, the ultimate in meaningful retirement. I never would have believed you'd take an early retirement, but that just shows you what I knew about God's plans. I want you to know that you showed us so much about what our priorities should be. You loved your Lord, in a quiet, daily way that meant you were never afraid to be honest or helpful even when it wasn't comfortable or convenient. I remember. I'm trying to live like that too.

So, Lord, keep me following in the steps of both of my fathers, my dear earthly one, and you, my dearer eternal one. Take my hand and help me learn daily how to live for you, how to live awake because the time is short, and how to not fear death nor ignore it. It is coming for me too, but with you Savior, as my guide, may we walk together to that far shore, where there is weeping no more.

Your Turn—This chapter was taken directly from one of my journals. I used the process of writing to help me face my grief. I also used it later to remember more and more about my dad so I could pass on detailed stories to the four granddaughters he barely knew. Do you have someone you need to grieve over? Do you have fears about death you need to face? God longs to hear your pain and to help you work through it to peace.

The Creative Project Journal

There are different kinds of gifts, but the same Spirit. There are different kinds of service, but the same Lord. There are different kinds of working, but the same God works all of them in all men.

1 Corinthians 12:4-6

Creativity is an awesome word. It makes me think of Einstein or Edison or the principal of our grade school who can't even write his Christmas letter without turning it into something amazingly original. Yet creativity also means just looking at something in a new way, figuring out a replacement ingredient in a recipe, or how to slice cheese with a credit card at a picnic where no one remembered a knife. Creativity is not only for geniuses. Let me repeat that. *Creativity is not only for geniuses.*

Sometimes when I taught Creative Writing to junior high students, I teased them by saying, "If you bore me, you'll get an F." Actually, I gave out no Fs, and very few Ds, because I longed for my students to recognize the fun of writing. Fun isn't found in cliches, in rehashing old plot lines, and in rainbow/kitten type poems. It's found in being creative, in being the surprising, original you that God created. When you are yourself, that's entertainment! You don't have to be super intelligent to be creative either. I believe all of us have the capacity to think up new ideas, to consider new perspectives; but it takes three qualities: time, concentration and courage.

Creative people ponder. I remember sitting on a couch in my college dorm room for an hour trying to think of an idea. A professor had asked me to design the cover for a class-compiled set of art teaching plans. I sat,

I stood, I paced, and I sat some more. I knew I didn't have the artistic ability to make a visual impact. My professor knew that too. So why had he asked me? Maybe he knew that what I lacked in artistry I usually made up for in creativity. That's exactly what I needed, a creative idea that would epitomize my feelings about the teaching of art. Okay, so what are your feelings, Ramona?

That's the stewing I did, the pondering. It took time, and it took concentration. Once in a while I'd jump up for a scratch piece of paper and scribble something down, but I always crumbled it up, because I knew I hadn't captured "The Idea" yet. I needed some special clothing for my gut feeling to wear, and I knew I'd recognize it when it came to me.

Then it came—like a gift my subconscious handed to me because of my hour of patient concentration. I would picture the magic of creativity as a strange, vegetable-like castle. It would be encircling and choking the typical drawing kids make (when they're not encouraged to be creative) of a square house with a triangle roof and an apple tree in the back yard. I grabbed up a pencil and sketched it. I liked it. No, it wasn't great art, but it symbolized a great idea, that imaginative drawing will choke out children's habitual, boring drawings if encouraged.

Looking back, I have to smile a little at my enthusiasm. I still think it wasn't a bad idea, but I'm not sure many of my classmates got what I was driving at. (Often I erred in the direction of obscurity in those days.) Yet even if I would change the drawing, I wouldn't change the process of getting that idea. I still use it today. I have faith in it, in fact, because it has worked for me so often. I gather my materials, my research, my thoughts, and then I ponder. I consider what my goals are, who my audience is, and how I might reach them; and then I wait. Eventually, an idea worthy of my project comes to me, sometimes after an hour, sometimes not for days or weeks, but it comes. It always comes. I've used the process to write essays, to get myself unlost, to help my children with their problems, to write this book.

My idea for that cover design, however, would never have come to me if I'd given into my fears: "He'll think it's dumb!" "I call this art?" "Everybody's going to laugh or call me weird!" It takes courage to stand by our creative ideas, because they often seem strange, even threatening at first. That's what makes them creative. Jesus was the most creative human being who ever lived. He threatened everyone's status quo, their lifestyles. He forced them to face the issue: Do we change our perspective or die in our own "righteousness?"

Some people will automatically assume that new is bad. "And when the demon was driven out, the man who had been dumb spoke. The crowd was amazed and said, 'Nothing like this has ever been seen in Israel.' But the Pharisees said, 'It is by the prince of demons that he drives out demons'" (Matthew 9:33,34). If you believe in your idea, if after prayer, advice and consideration, it still seems true, wise and helpful, ignore the people who throw cold water on you. Given enough time, they may become your most ardent supporters—when *your* idea becomes the status quo.

Emerson once said, "Ideas must work through the brains and the arms of good and brave men, or they are no better than dreams." So pinning down those dreams, developing them, is the hard part. No, that's misleading. It's only hard because it takes day-by-day self-discipline. Actually, it's also the easy part, because once you get past the huge wall of fear and traditionalism to a good idea, it's only a long stairway upwards to your destination. You get to travel there step by step. All you need, therefore, is a road map, an architectural drawing, a treasure map to follow to your dream. That's where your journal comes in. It can be your road map.

I call this special kind of journal a Creative Project Journal. It can be used for anything. Use it to plan an interior decorating scheme, to discover your life's ambi-

138

tions, to reveal your personality strengths, to write your novel, to organize your thoughts on gardening, to sketch a made-up cartoon character, to chart your spiritual love odyssey, to calm down your home life, to plan your rummage sale. Use it for anything and everything! It's a notebook where you collect all the odds and ends of notes, research, ideas, lists, timetables, charts, anecdotes, drawings, to save them until you're ready to put it all together into a plan of action, into a book, into a personality change.

In your creative project journal, you record your best ideas. You can be your most creative. Nobody can shoot them down because nobody sees them—yet. You have room to move in, to prune here, to replant there, to throw out what doesn't work. It's freedom and playfulness between two covers.

There are two basic types of creative project journals: organic and organized. Organic journals are bound or spiral books you keep as the mood moves you. They have no form. You simply add ideas, scribblings, sketches, as they occur to you. From front to back, they will be formless and exciting. 'You get to see practical steps right beside a dream you had about the project. Such juxtaposing can be mind-stimulating in itself.

Organic journals can frustrate you, however, because you can't easily see your progress and may have difficulty locating a tidbit you need at once. Plus, since the weeds and wheat are all growing together, later you must expect a ruthless harvest. Chemist Linus Pauling (a Nobel Peace Prize winner) said: "The trick to having good ideas is to come up with a lot of ideas and then throw the bad ones out."

Despite its drawbacks, this type of creative project journal is my favorite. It's intuitive and surprising, which appeals to my mind. For this book, I kept an organic journal. Sometimes I worried that I'd never get the chapters into any kind of meaningful order, because I wrote them so haphazardly. My organized husband chuckled at my approach, but I must tell you that never in my life have I felt such joy in working on a long project.

If you are more of a term paper type person, who likes numbered notecards and knowing exactly where you stand, you may feel much more comfortable with an organized creative project journal. It allows you to have the same exuberant ideas but it also allows you to put them in some kind of order right away. Choose a 3-ring binder for your project and lots of dividers with those colorful cellophane tabs. Then simply divide your project into meaningful sections like Research, Timetables, Plan of Action, Materials, Miscellaneous, etc. You can fill those sections methodically one at a time, or as the spirit moves you. You may lose some of the surprising freshness on the page and the crazy, playful feel of the organic journal, but you gain easy reference and the constant assurance that you are covering all the bases.

Journal writing often gets accused of being time-wasting, ego-centric. I don't believe that. To me, all journal writing is mind-expanding and spiritually nourishing; but sometimes doubts do creep in, especially when the wash baskets are full, and I can feel grit under my feet. That's when I turn to my creative project journal. In it, I know I'm using my ideas to make a difference, to change my life. My creative project journal fairly shouts, "Give me a lever long enough, and I can move the world."

Your Turn—Make a list of creative projects you've been putting off. They may be as practical as planning a rummage sale or a craft fair for your Ladies Society, or they may be more idealistic like starting your own in-home business or learning how to witness to your neighbors. Choose one project that keeps nagging at you: "Come on. Give me a chance to grow into something wonderful." Then, in a separate notebook (organic or organized), begin now to gather ideas and notes to set your creativity free.

THE TABLET OF SHARING

You may never create a masterpiece, never win a Pulitzer Prize or a magazine writer's award—you may never even be discovered by a small town publisher. But, like Grandma Moses, you may be an "artist" just the same—you will have made use of the gift of creativity that no creature other than the human beings enjoy. You will have put your thoughts, your experiences, or your dreams on paper where someone else sometime may read them. That's writing! And that is in itself a great achievement. Whatever publishers, editors or critics— or the man or woman next door—may say, you're a writer. And never forget it.

Leonard L. Knott
Writing for the Joy of It

M emoirs of a Dishwasher

You know, they straightened out the
Mississippi River in places, to make room
for houses and liveable acreage.
Occasionally the river floods these places.
"Floods" is the word they use, but in fact it is
not flooding; it is remembering.
Remembering where it used to be. All water
has a perfect memory and is forever trying
to get back to where it was. Writers are like
that: remembering where we were, what
valley we ran through, what the banks were
like, the light that was there and the route
back to our original place. It is emotional
memory—what the nerves and the skin
remember as well as how it appeared. And
a rush of imagination is our "flooding."

Toni Morrison
The Site of Memory

I stack the dirty dishes to the left of my sinks. The
counters are clear everywhere else. Ready, set, go—I
begin to wash. This is an old, old ritual hardly changed
for nine years: the way I drop the silverware in first so
it slips to the bottom, hidden beneath mounds of bubbles to be washed last (rewarding me near the end with
its sheen); the way I swirl my cloth around the insides
of cereal bowls, my ungloved fingers, hot and red, feeling with tips and fingernails for sticking particles of
Wheaties; the way I push my cloth harder around the
rims of our tea mugs, slippery from our sipping; and
the way I swish out popcorn kernels and swollen mac-
aroni noodles before I wash the pans, because I loathe

the feel of things bumping into my hands, like strange fish with tiny sucking mouths. Nine years and I do it almost the same as ever. I think of the decades that may be left to me and all of the dishes still to be washed. It is almost comforting—some things won't change. I will always do dishes.

As I wash, memories come to me. I remember once when I broke two glasses in one session at the sink. What wonder I felt at the quiet red drops spreading out in the water. Hurry, stop the bleeding and fish out the shards. Drain the water. Get a paper bag. Do I have all of the pieces? Tiny slivers wink up at me from the bottom of the shiny plug. I shake them too into the bag. There, all hidden in the morning garbage. Just another clinking bag. Then in a few days or weeks, Larry will mutter, "We sure seem low on glasses lately." "Don't we!" I'll say brightly and suck on the finger of my deceit.

My mind makes frequent small journeys like that one as I wash. No one bothers me, perhaps because they're afraid I might ask for help, but also because this early evening time is precious to all of them. They use it for unwinding with the paper or T.V., for reunions with sisters they couldn't nag or tease all day, for sloshing in snow or rolling in grass or flying down streets on their bikes, for curling up with a book, or for tinkling on the piano. Usually I don't mind being alone. I like the solitude. I like bringing my dishes back into cleanliness while my mind wanders where it wants.

I think about my own sisters and the dishwashing we never got to do. I'll do that differently. By next year, or surely the year after, my two older girls can take this job from me, or at least stand on the linoleum floor beside me and move in this rhythmic dance from sink to counter to cupboard. I never got to know my mother's plates intimately. Silly as it sounds, that makes me sad. I don't know where she even kept her Tupperware, or her stoneware, or that china with the leafy swirls around the edges that seemed to spell magically my dad's name, Dick. I saw our dishes selfishly as simply holders of my food, never as things I must treat kindly, bathing them and placing them reverently in their resting places. If I had offered more often to help, I wonder if my mother finally would have accepted. Instead, I used her competence as an excuse for my laziness.

The thought of laziness makes me speed up my washing. I'm certainly not lazy now, but was I then? Maybe. Partly afraid, too, that I'd never be able to do the job well enough to please her, constricted by the thought I might break some stemware and gather her scorn to me. No, I wasn't very trusting. This thought brings some more memories.

There *were* some things I helped with. I remember helping Dad bring home his small sailboat after every excursion on the lake. We'd wash it in the backyard with ice water from the hose, balancing it awkwardly between us like a banana-colored whale. I can still hear the splashing echo of that water hitting inside the hull and the bright color gleaming out as the sand was jettisoned away. Then between just the two of us we'd have to carry it into the garage and lift it onto two hanging ropes, swaying from the rafters like jungle vines. As we grunted and sweated, I remember wondering if the clean-up process was worth the hours on the lake of tacking and stalling and trailing fingers in the silky waters. It must have been, because whenever Dad asked the next time, "Want to go sailing?" I always said, "Sure."

That sailboat of course reminds me of still more memories, but I believe you have the idea. Being quiet and alone at the sink encourages remembering. That is also what your journal will do for you. Being quiet and alone with a pen in your hand encourages your memories to surface. Let it all come flooding back to you: your first love interest, the games your family played, the arguments, the make-ups, the significance of plates and sailboats. Why not even let your journal become the autobiography of your life?

Don't say you're too young yet or have led a boring life. You've already had a life full of emotions, growth and sensations. You've felt the excitement and fear of having your long hair cut for the first time. You remember the first time someone hit you or called you a terrible name. You remember the soft fur in your hands of a pet you cherished. Write about all that. Also write about your internal life, about what God has changed in you and what he is working on now. Who says it has to be all organized and chronological like a published autobiography? Just capture the past as you reel it on the line of your thought.

Of course you could organize it. You could write it in a chronological order or you could be more fresh and pick a theme, something that expresses your individuality: journeys I have made and why, the tree in my backyard and how we grew together, churches I have known. Or write your memoirs as an interview with yourself. Or write two stories at the same time, your today story and all the yesterdays leading up to today, moving back and forth between them as ideas occur to you. Or write the story of your life as a series of letters to a friend, or arrange it by seasons, or write about your life-long relationship with your grandmother. If you are using the loose-leaf journal I described in chapter 1, you could even have a whole section just for remembering the past.

Be creative and do it for fun, but make sure it honestly reveals the real you, not the one you wish everybody could know, but the one you and your Lord already know. Pack it full of sights, sounds, tastes, smells and the feel of what has moved you, what has stuck with you all these years. Autobiography never used to interest me much, but now it is one of my favorite kinds of reading and my favorite kind of writing. After all, don't the writing teachers say, "Write what you know"? The subject you know best, and can write most revealingly about, is of course yourself. Plunge in, feel the water, let the memories come flooding in.

Your Turn—On your idea page at the front of your journal add words that remind you of some of your favorite memories. Those words should jostle free even more memories until the list starts to become heavy with memoir possibilities. Keep jotting down ideas until you feel like writing, then start exploring all the yous of the past for insight into the you of now.

Journals as Alabaster Jars

And the house was filled with the fragrance of the perfume.

John 12:3

The woman poured out pure nard on Jesus' feet and wiped it with her hair. Though people snickered and grumbled at the waste, Jesus didn't. He recognized her unrestrained pouring out for what it was: this woman needed to give something intimate of herself to her Lord.

Mary could have wrapped the alabaster jar in Hallmark paper, handing it to Jesus with a card that read, "All the Best!" but instead she chose to get down on her knees and splash perfume over his feet with her own hands, washing off the inevitable grime and perspiration. Instead of rising then to find a linen towel, she wiped his feet dry with her own hair. This is not the action of a cool, detached observer. She loved her Creator and Savior and longed to express that love up close, intimately.

This scene probably embarrassed some of the disciples. Even I squirm a bit, thinking, "Would I have loved him enough to ignore everybody else like that? Do I want to get that close? Could I pour myself out as intimately as Mary did?"

Pouring yourself out honestly to God and to others is extremely difficult. By now you've written in your journal long enough to realize this. Many times, what you've written has been posturing, justifying, covering up. Only fleetingly have you been able with God's help to shine the light of truth on the page, but when it happened, how the words glowed and how you longed to do it again and again. You found the reward Paul speaks of in 2 Corinthians 2:14: "and through us spreads everywhere the fragrance of the knowledge of [Christ]."

I want you to notice something, however. Who else enjoyed the fragrance when Mary poured out her love for her soon-to-be-crucified Savior? The account says, "the house was filled with the fragrance." She influenced many others that day, shaking up their preconceived ideas about giving and sacrifice and real love. She made the whole house take notice and it lingered for some time, I'm sure. You see, when we pour out sacrificially, honestly and intimately, others have to notice because the fragrance is so strong and unusual.

Your journal can become an alabaster jar for someone other than yourself, too. From it, you can pour out intimate love for someone who needs to feel your love up close. I'm talking about writing a journal to a special person, recording daily your thoughts and emotions as if you spoke right to him or her. Yes, it might be embarrassing, and you have no guarantee someone won't snicker or grumble about how you wasted time and effort. You may have to kneel down humbly, admitting faults. You may have to wash away old problems and heartaches that have dirtied your relationship, and you may have to dry away what's left with the caressing honesty of your own feelings; but, friend, guess what will happen: "and the house was filled with the fragrance of the perfume."

I kept a journal one fall for my oldest sister. Debbie and I had always had a few links that helped us communicate: our fondness for writing, for books, and for talking about anything idealistic and deep. But distance and our different lifestyles had lately made it hard really to touch. We always seemed to be trying to talk around her barking dogs or my begging daughters or our husbands who needed some attention too. Once, after another frustrating visit, I wondered, "Does she really know who I am?"

I longed to give her more of an idea of how much she meant to me, to let her glimpse some of my memories of her as "big sister," and to bring her into my everyday life and musings. What better way, I decided, than to write to her as I had written so often in my journal. Also, it just might make a treasured (yet inexpensive) Christmas gift.

I started in September, with good intentions to be done by November 30. Come the end of November, almost half of the book stared at me blankly. Now the choice: do I send it unfinished, tear the pages out (what sacrilege!) or put on the steam and write reams every day until December 15, the last possible day I could hope to mail it in time for Christmas? I decided to go for it.

Perhaps procrastination was even a good thing in this case. I didn't have time to think too carefully about what I was writing to Debbie. I included quotes I liked, things the girls said that were funny or illuminating, poems that jumped into my head. I wrote pages and pages about thoughts that occurred to me, without censoring or editing. I didn't have time to care. What came of all that scribbling was a book unique and sometimes messy, but loaded down with love. I had spent two weeks talking to my sister on paper. I let her into my mind and heart. Sometimes I worried that I'd told her too much. "What's she going to think about this dumb idea?" I'd worry; but then I realized that, even if it was a dumb idea, she'd feel good that I trusted her enough to be vulnerable in front of her.

When you give someone a part of you that is as intimate as a journal, you are vulnerable. You take a big risk. They could kick you as you kneel in front of them pouring out your heart. They could laugh or gossip about what you've told them, or worse yet, ignore your offering and put it on a closet shelf. But you can't touch them, anoint them with your love, unless you risk that rejection.

I will tell you how my sister reacted. On Christmas Day she called. "Monie," she said with tears in her voice, "I've never been given a gift that meant so much to me." She had read part of it already and planned to curl up nightly and savor small bits at a time. Now that's embarrassing, if I think too hard about it, because what I'd just jotted down were inarticulate first thoughts. I couldn't go back and delete or copy edit, so what she was reading certainly wasn't "literature," and often not even sensible.

Yet I do know why she loved lt. She loved it for the same reason that I would treasure a similar book from her. It would symbolize time, effort and intimacy— three elements of true love. If people do not take time and effort and reveal themselves to you, they don't love you. That's sacrifice, the giving up of self, the sharing of the tiny moments we usually waste on ourselves solely. She knew it didn't take months, like knitting an afghan, but she also knew it took courage and love. She knew I was bending over in front of her humbly, hoping she'd appreciate my out-pouring.

I challenge you to allow a journal of yours to become an alabaster jar for someone. Choose a person, if you can, who would especially be surprised and moved by such a gift, who may even be changed by it. You don't need to plan the whole journal, although it does help to choose a few things to write about ahead of time. Don't be afraid to throw in poems, songs and quotes from others to round out your journal. They show your thinking, too, and certainly enrich the journal. Do anything that you like and that your loved one might like. Then wrap it up and send it off.

Giving isn't easy, not true giving. You may even feel a strong urge to keep the book to yourself. That's like never letting a baby be born. It was created for a special purpose, fashioned in love. Let it emerge! I can't predict what will happen or how it will be received, but I will predict what happens inside of you because of your giving. You will have grown in humility and honesty. The next time, it will be easier yet to give of yourself sacrificially, to pour out for others, and you will also reap another reward.

This is our reward—joy in service, joy in the Lord! As Paul said, "But even if I am being poured out like a drink offering on the sacrifice and service coming from your faith, I am glad and rejoice with all of you. So you too should be glad and rejoice with me" (Philippians 2:17,18). Though we are poured out, we are filled up with Christ's abundant blessings. Let us rejoice.

Your Turn—In your present journal, plan now for whom you will soon start a journal. Write about why this person may appreciate such a gift, what you might write about, and your feelings concerning honesty and intimacy. Face your fears and your embarrassment and turn them over to Jesus. Lay them at his feet in humility and love.

Once upon a Miracle

Do not forget the things your eyes have seen or let them slip from your heart as long as you live. Teach them to your children and to their children after them.

Deuteronomy 4:9

Come closer. Let me tell you a story. It's about how you can gather your children around you with up-turned faces eager to hear God's word. Sound pretty far-fetched? It's not, because everyone loves a story, and children especially love to hear about that magical time "before you were born." You have a rich source of story material to draw on: "what your eyes have seen." Sharing stories about how you've seen God move in your life will make your family's devotion time glow with meaning. I used to buy all the latest devotion books. Yes, my children liked them and listened polite-ly, but something seemed missing. One of the problems was finding a book right for all four of them, not too simple nor too complex. But the other problem was more subtle, how to find stories that spoke to their hearts?

It's not that the devotions weren't well-written, it's just that they weren't written for *my* children. Then one day, after a particularly sterile devotion time when all four of them seemed more interested in the exploits of a spider on the ceiling, I thought, "Well, why not just tell them how God has worked in my life?"

For several months now, I've been doing just that. It's not as difficult as you might think. First, I decided what understandings I wanted them to come to, such as the power of prayer or the sacrificial aspects of love. Then I picked Bible passages and stories to read or tell to them that supported these understandings.

Lastly, to bring all we'd learned together, I told a story from my own life. I talked about how I saw the power of prayer when praying for help on an empty highway about a flat tire that couldn't be changed, and how help came. I talked about how I sacrificed ungrudgingly once, and how later, undeservedly, I reaped a wonderful reward. Sometimes I told stories they couldn't remember about their early childhood days, and somehow no spiders on the ceiling ever bothered us again.

Telling them stories of how Jesus had guided me, how he had taken my sins and troubles and changed them into lessons and blessings, ignited their minds. They bubbled over with stories of their own, often revealing problems or feelings that may never have surfaced if I hadn't shared first: "Remember when you told us about that policeman being like an angel from heaven? I could use a police-angel on the bus lately." "I gave her that last piece of cake, Mom, even though I didn't want to. Sacrificial love sure is hard!" All of us became more comfortable talking about the spiritual side of our everyday lives.

A surprising benefit was that not being tied to a devotion book brought me face to face with my daughters. As I talked, I could see flickers of confusion, embarrassment or tenderness. I could tell exactly when to explain something more clearly, move on, or when to ask a probing question. I became their tutor, their sounding board, their grownup friend. Reading someone else's stories could never duplicate what we found, curled up on a twin bed in the twilight.

You can use your journal for this very special purpose—to remember those stories on paper so that when you need to pull one out, it's there just for the taking. You can also keep a children's devotions journal, solely for writing down the outlines or word for word messages you want to say to them. Let your children see you putting journal writing to use for their eternal good.

Perhaps this idea isn't for everyone. But for mothers and fathers hungry to teach their children the practical truths of the Bible so they not only listen but keep them in their hearts as long as they live, try it. Don't be afraid or think it difficult. Just gather them around you and plunge in: "Once upon a miracle, Jesus changed my life. . . ."

Your Turn—Practice writing a few devotion plans. Think of an understanding you long for your children—or someone else's children—to have. Search your Bible for stories and passages that support this understanding. Then think of a story from your own life that also supports what God teaches. Write it down in your journal in detail, recalling your emotions, colors, smells, anything that will bring it alive for young listeners. Also, jot down a few questions to get them thinking about stories to tell to you.

The Tablet of My Heart

*The good man brings good things out
of the good stored up in his heart, and the
evil man brings evil things out of the evil
stored up in his heart. For out of the overflow of his heart his mouth speaks.*

Luke 6:45

For many years I've come before my Lord with pen in
hand. I've opened my Bible, my notebook and my
heart. Have all those hours of scribbling been worth it?
If you've tried some of the suggestions in this book,
maybe you can answer. Until you do try some spiritual
journal writing, nothing I can say in these last para-
graphs will convince you. Only by *doing* can you really
comprehend the satisfaction that keeps me writing—
and the joy.

I can't resist mentioning, however, one last reason to
keep writing. People like to say, "You are what you eat,"
or, "You are what you read." I believe it's also true that
"you are what you dwell on." Our minds seethe daily
with thoughts, our hearts with feelings. The ones we
allow ourselves to dwell on begin to come back again
and again, and soon they even influence our actions.
This is probably why Paul urges us in Philippians 4:8 to
dwell on whatever is true and noble.

Unfortunately, when we dwell on evil things, they too
influence our actions. I know this from my own life. I
remember one time when a woman hurt me with some
unkind comments to my employer. Though I wanted to
love her and let God's forgiving nature be seen through
me, I also gave in to the temptation to do some harm-
less fantasizing, to review her comments repeatedly,

making up my own needling and brutally honest responses. Of course, I'd never *say* those things, I assured myself. The next day when I showed up for work, I even breathed a quick prayer, "Please, Lord, help me speak as you would speak." What I did say, however, what slipped out against my will and good intentions, were the very sarcastic words I'd practiced over and over in my mind. I became what I had dwelled on.

I've learned to use my journals to help me dwell on the things of God. How badly I need that daily practice to reign in my unruly mind and heart. As I write, I can almost sense my Savior looking over my shoulder, sometimes nodding in understanding, sometimes slightly frowning. I babble on like a trusting child, knowing that he loves me no matter what I write or do, but that he'll also try to lead me to the good he has stored up in my heart.

Jesus is my leader, the ruler of my soul and body, but to understand what that means I must remain close to his word. I must read it, dwell on it, and apply it to my everyday decisions, just as David did. "I have considered my ways and have turned my steps to your statutes" (Psalm 119:59). If I do that, it's inevitable that I will reap blessings: "Blessed are they who keep his statutes and seek him with all their heart" (Psalm 119:2).

No matter whether you keep a journal or not, you've already discovered the blessings of believing in Jesus. You know that no matter how ungrateful and cruel you are, he still loves you and died for those very sins. You have eternal life, not because you deserve it, but because Jesus rescued you from what you deserve. Now, even on your blackest days, your heart rests in this wondrous knowledge. You know God! Isn't it amazing that he has allowed you to know him?

What you may not know yet is the everyday peace that comes from trusting in that knowledge, looking for God to control your mind and heart. "Those who live in accordance with the Spirit have their minds set on what the Spirit desires. The mind of sinful man is death, but the mind controlled by the Spirit is life and peace" (Romans 8:5,6).

That's why I keep a journal, to hand over control of my life bit by bit to Jesus. The Devil tempts me to say, "Hey, wait a minute. I have to figure this out—worry, plan, act—or everything will fall apart!"

Quite the opposite is true. When I try to worry and control things, when I stop dwelling on God's Word and dwell instead on my own machinations, things get bleak and tangled. Graciously, Jesus turns me back towards him each time I buy a new notebook, bow my head and pour out my heart. I tell him, then, "Lord, I'm sorry. Thank You for your eternal patience with me. I ask You again to stand beside me and teach me what I need so much to learn." And that, dear brother or sister in Christ, is what journal writing is all about. Out of the overflow of your heart, your pen will speak.

Your Turn—I have no more assignments for you. It's time to continue journal writing because you want to, not because you're trying to learn to want to. It's time to make your journal peculiarly yours. Make up your own assignment. Tomorrow make up another one. Until you do this, keeping a spiritual journal will only be an idea you borrowed from me. I don't want that anymore. It's an idea big enough for all of us, for millions of variations, and I bequeath you your variation right now. You have read a whole book about the tablet of my heart. The next book you hold in your hand, I pray, will be the tablet of your own heart. May God be with you.